THE TANTRIC PATH
—TO—
HIGHER CONSCIOUSNESS

Male Within Female
Enlightenment Made Manifest
Om Mane Padme Hum

THE TANTRIC PATH TO HIGHER CONSCIOUSNESS

Jewel in the Lotus

A Complete and Systematic Course in Tantric Kriya Yoga

SUNYATA SARASWATI
BODHI AVINASHA

New Age Books

ISBN: 81-7822-237-x

First Indian Edition: Delhi, **2006**
First Published: U.S.A., 1987
Revised Edition: U.S.A., 1996
Earlier published under the title '*Jewel in the Lotus: The Tantric Path to Higher Consciousness*'

Illustrated by Ty Keller

Disclaimer:

Tantric Kriya Yoga is a system of practices promoting health and well-being. Caution and common sense should be used in following any of the suggestions about food, exercise, sexual activity, etc. This course is not meant to replace competent medical advice. Anyone suffering from venereal disease or any local illness of their sexual organs should consult a medical doctor before practicing the methods taught here.

For more information contact:
TANTRIKA INTERNATIONAL,
12115 Magnolia Blvd.
PMB # 143, Valley Village, CA, 91607.

Published by
NEW AGE BOOKS
A-44 Naraina Phase-I
New Delhi-110 028 (INDIA)
Email: nab@vsnl.in
Website: www.newagebooksindia.com

For Sale in Asia Only

Printed in India
at Shri Jainendra Press
A-45 Naraina Phase-I, New Delhi-110 028

CONTENTS

INTRODUCTION TO REVISED EDITION

We are delighted to present this revised edition of our basic Tantric text. When the book was first written, almost ten years ago, Tantra was practically unknown in this culture. In the years that intervened, Tantra has become well-known, featured with cover stories in every new age publication. We were pleased to be on the forefront of that awakening.

The first edition presented many powerful techniques which traditionally had only been available within an ashram setting, under the close supervision of a master. Realizing that those techniques, in their full power, could prove to be too intense for most people as beginners, we didn't tell the whole truth. By leaving out a step, or doing something backwards, you lose the effect of the technique. This is how much of the work was presented.

If someone were serious about the practice, and did the modified version with some dedication, he would eventually be instructed by his inner guidance and find himself doing it properly. One who was not pure in heart, or was not ready, wouldn't receive such guidance until his time was right. In this way, we made the knowledge available without putting anyone at risk.

In this revised edition, we have clarified these obfuscations, since there are many people who are now mature enough spiritually to handle the work. Once again, we rely on a self-selection process and assume only those who are ready will be interested enough to follow through.

Questions that have been raised, through those years, from users of the book, have prompted us to rewrite certain portions, with greater clarity and consistency.

The changes in this edition are often very subtle, and would only be noticed by one who had made a deep study of the materials. But they make a great difference in the effect of the practice.

In our first edition, we self-published, knowing absolutely nothing about how to do that. Somehow the book came together, and now is available in German, French, Spanish and Polish. It is in progress in Czech, Hungarian, Bulgarian, Slovenian and Italian. Thousands of lives have been touched by this work, even in its humble presentation. We are now thrilled to move into a beautiful and professional "look" which will attract even more people to a practice that will transform their lives.

PREFACE

Rarely does a published work of consummate stature, written with such sensitivity and openness to truth, satisfy our growing need for answers and preparation on the spiritual path. *The Tantric Path to Higher Consciousness* is clearly this exceptional contribution to the Tantric Yoga tradition—for all students, beginners and advanced.

I have found in it a cornucopia of exploration which has accelerated my spiritual progress to the heights promised in all the great spiritual teachings.

I am sure the readers will join with me in attesting to the lifelong blessings this study will surely unfold.

—*Timothy Vanech*

HOW TO USE THIS BOOK

We are pleased to acknowledge you as one of a small group of spiritual seekers who are drawn to the Tantric path. Sunyata has a wealth of knowledge to share with you, gathered over many years from the far corners of the earth. This is the first time in America that these secret teachings have been made available, independent of the religious and philosophical belief systems.

The techniques presented here are some of the most powerful tools ever given to man to aid his growth. Any one of the techniques, if fully mastered, would be enough to utterly transform your consciousness. Many major religious movements have sprung up using just one or two of these techniques as their basis. Of course, they require a considerable financial investment and your allegiance to a guru or tradition before revealing these carefully guarded secrets. The techniques you will receive produce powerful results, without guru worship, proving that you can access your own inner guru, can be the master of your destiny.

From the vast body of knowledge that makes up Tantric Kriya Yoga, we have distilled 12 lessons that provide a systematic development of your understanding and experience. Each lesson consists of four parts:

- A discussion of esoteric principles;
- Yogic techniques for a direct experience of these principles;
- Sexual practices which implement these principles;
- Suggested ways to bring these principles into your every day life so that each moment becomes part of your spiritual practice.

This course is highly condensed. Each lesson, if fully elaborated, would fill several books. We assume you have already read such books and are still not clear about incorporating the knowledge into your life.

This is an advanced course. We assume you have tried meditation, have been on a spiritual path, have had some experience of etheric energies. If not, this course will probably have little meaning for you. Begin the practice and take your time.

This is not a book on sex therapy. All the sex research done in this country deals with dysfunction. There is very little attention given to those who function "normally" but still feel that something is missing. This course will teach you about transcendent sex, the ultimate expression of your sexuality.

Scan the whole course to get an overview. Then come back and focus on one lesson at a time. Stay with a lesson as long as is necessary to feel a mastery of the material. Set your own pace.

It is important to establish a regular time for your practice. Give yourself just half an hour every day to check in with your source, to attune your body and mind to your highest wisdom. The benefits are beyond your expectations. Be consistent with the practice long enough to experience that for yourself.

A Word of Caution: These practices were kept secret through the ages because most people were not ready for Unity Consciousness. Particularly in our Western culture, almost everyone is badly fragmented.

The practice of Tantra will amplify whatever disturbance is present in your sub-conscious, until it has been brought into consciousness and resolved. This is why the tradition has not been written down. It's better if someone is there to guide you through the rough parts when repressed material begins to surface, someone who has been through psychological clearing and understands what is happening. If it gets too intense, you might want to find a sensitive therapist. In the past there has been a guru to safeguard the disciple, but you will be on your own. Contact the Ashram if you need help.

Above all, <u>don't try to avoid repressed material as it comes up.</u> These techniques are some of the most potent ever devised to stir up the subconscious and force banished memories into consciousness. If you refuse to handle the material, you might set up an intense psychological conflict, which could even trigger a psychotic break. We are dealing with very powerful techniques to activate very powerful energies. They must be handled with great respect.

Join the Ashram. There are people all over the world who resonate to this work, a spiritual family who nurture and encourage each other in this path. Take advantage of the guidance that's available from people who have opened up this frontier, who have realized the enormous benefits of this practice, far beyond anything they had hoped for. Know that you are not alone in your journey.

Get the Cobra Breath Initiation. This technique, a long held secret, is the key to mastering your sexual energies. The time has come when this knowledge must come out of the hidden mystery schools and be available to any who would hear it. The time for caution is over. We are told repeatedly by the masters that unless mankind makes an enormous leap in consciousness in the very near future, life on this planet is in jeopardy. Take the knowledge and use it. Become a beacon in the darkness.

Lesson 1

Enlightenment Through Tantric Kriya Yoga

Yoga is the Science of Expanding Consciousness. The Eastern view of the nature of man is very different from the Western. In the East, they see man at one with God and with the Universe. They understand that ultimately man is that Universal Intelligence or Consciousness that supports life in this Universe.

Man's basic problem is simply that he has forgotten his true nature, has become entangled in the drama of being an individual, striving for individual recognition, achievement, satisfaction. Man feels separate, alienated, at odds with his world only because he has lost sight of his essential truth. Enlightenment is simply rising above this limited self-concept, returning to that basic unity that has always been, and realizing the light within.

Therefore, the problem is not one of learning enough or achieving enough to pull ourselves out of our present state of inadequacy, as the Western mind has been conditioned to believe. It is simply a problem of perceiving the truth as it is, without distortion. In higher states of consciousness we are more aware of the universe and our place in it.

The solution is one of perception. Our ability to perceive depends on the sensitivity of our nervous system. For thousands of years Yogis have experimented with techniques to manipulate the nervous system, to extend its functional range, to allow consciousness to expand. Yoga is the science that has grown out of these experiments.

Enlightenment is a return to the Source that created you, becoming aware of the Source of your energy, becoming one with that Source. Life energy on this planet comes from somewhere in the center of the Milky Way. Yogic techniques presented in this course will allow you to experience this for yourself. As if you had turned on a color TV in your mind's eye, you can see, deep in the cavities within your brain, the vast Milky Way. Once you have contacted this energy and returned from that expanded state, you will never be the same.

Tantra Yoga is the Sexual Path, a vast and ancient system of rituals and practical techniques which use the great creative energy of sexual passion to propel you into higher consciousness. The rites and rituals are very powerful.

The word "Tantra" comes from the Sanskrit "tanoti" — to expand" and "trayati" — "liberation." To expand consciousness, to liberate us from the physical level of our being, we use the five senses to their limit and then go beyond that limit. Tantra teaches you to explore every aspect of your consciousness. You first open the consciousness of the brain, awakening countless dormant brain cells, which expands the five senses and then transforms every other aspect of your body/mind.

Many modern yoga schools improperly teach that we should sublimate our senses in striving for transcendent truth. They frown on sexuality, arguing that it distracts seekers from the goal of samadhi or enlightenment. They try to subdue and suppress sexual desire, making an ideal of celibacy. Many yogic schools teach that ascetic renunciation and withdrawal from life is the only means to Truth.

But this is only because they don't understand sexual energy and how to use it to achieve their aim. The truth is that spiritual and sexual energy are two sides of the same coin – the upward flowing spiritual energy "becomes" sexual when it turns down. Tantra recognizes that the common householder is not inclined toward renunciation. Rather than subjugate the energy, Tantra redirects it and uses it to our advantage. Then its power becomes a blessing, and celibacy becomes irrelevent – a matter of personal choice.

Many spiritual schools and our western culture in general, have a deeply embedded conviction that sexuality is somehow evil and debased. They teach you must choose between "God and flesh." But they forgot that God is in the flesh and can be, indeed is to be found there for full realization. You will be greatly relieved to discover you don't have to choose – God is sexual pleasure, used rightly. Now the secrets of Tantra, which have been forced underground for hundreds of years by religions, "moralists" and the like, are coming to the surface as a vital and joyful means to enlightenment.

Transcendence through Sex. Tantra is not a license for sexual abandon, as the practice requires great discipline. The systems of Tantric Yoga use the most powerful energy that we know — sexual energy — to penetrate spiritual realms. The tantric masters discovered that prolonged sexual union produces supersensitivity to the energies in and around the lovers. Rather than turning away from the "illusions" of physical existence, tantric Yogis enter that physical dimension totally. Mastering their awareness of that level, they can expand their awareness to the next level and follow the path of ecstasy to the highest levels of human perfection.

Returning to the Cosmic Womb is the last initiation. A man is born with an erection and will die with an erection. In the time that intervenes, that sexual energy can transform him. Tantric methods are natural, life affirming, joyful. Every act becomes part of your spiritual practice. Tantra is sexuality in a spiritual context.

It takes enormous courage and dedication to be tantric in your view of sexuality. Our culture is very confused about sexuality. On one hand there are cultural pressures to inhibit your sexual expression. But you can never free yourself from sex by repressing it. Trying to avoid sex creates an obsession. Unexpressed sexual energy turns into neurosis and violence. We are enslaved by our sexuality and yet not permitted to enjoy it, so the hunger is never satisfied.

On the other hand, sex is thrown in your face in every magazine, movie, TV, etc. Gross sexuality in the media is rampant in our culture. But there is little support for the idea that sexuality is an expression of love which is sacred.

Love is the very essence of man, and yet how seldom it is manifest! Civilization has historically forbidden the expression of love by condemning sexuality. The contemporary world ignores love while exploiting sexuality. The Tantric must break the mold and defy the moral precept, for sex is the means by which we come to know love. LOVE IS SEX ENERGY TRANSFORMED. To know the elemental truth of love, you must first accept the divinity of sex and learn to worship through the senses, through the flesh. The more accepting you are of sex, the more free of it you become. Total acceptance and surrender to natural energies leads to the most sublime experiences.

History of Tantra. Tantra has always existed, for as long as man has wondered about the mystery of his existence and stood in awe of the primordial power of his sexual nature. Symbols of the Tantric heritage are found in every culture: in cave paintings from the Stone Age, in ancient Sumarian carvings, in magical texts from ancient Egypt, in mystical writings of the Hebrews and Greeks, and in the Arabian songs of love. The alchemy of medieval Europe disguised its tantric principles with romantic allegorical poetry. Paganism was based on the celebration of creative sexual energy. In many cultures, representations of the male and female genitals (lingam and yoni in Sanskrit) are widely displayed and revered for the creative power they represent.

It is unfortunately true that power can corrupt, and the powerful principles of Tantra have, in the wrong hands, been used in company with witchcraft, superstition, orgies, drinking blood, sado-masochism, black magic, human sacrifice and contact with evil spirits through decomposing bodies in cemeteries. But any powerful tool can be misused. That doesn't mean we should destroy all the tools!

Tantric practice has also inspired the best art and poetry of India, Arabia and China. Temples of India are covered with carvings of deities in every possible position of sexual union (which is a great embarrassment to the repressed Indian culture today).

It appears Tantra was once a worldwide spiritual practice, a common thread running through all civilizations. Hindus in India developed a system to balance male and female energies which strongly influenced the Taoists in China, the Buddhists in Tibet and all other Eastern religions.

Tantric teachings were closely guarded, transmitted orally from master to disciple, only after a long period of preparation and purification. Even when the tradition was finally written down in the 3rd Century, its meaning was obscured in allegory and symbols so only the initiates could understand. The secrets were guarded as protection from misuse, but also to give royalty and priesthood a tremendous power advantage over the masses.

The 11th and 12th centuries were the Golden Age of Tantra when it was practiced widely and openly in India. But the Moslem invasion in the 13th Century brought slaughter of all Tantrics and wholesale destruction of all manuscripts. The movement was forced underground where it has continued ever since. It had been preserved in remote monasteries, primarily in Tibet, but the recent Communist invasion of Tibet repeated the slaughter and attempt to stamp out Tantric practice. Tantrikas are threatening to those who would wield power. One who has realized his true nature cannot be subjugated to the will of a religious or political power structure.

By the Yogi calendar we are now in the final stage of a debased age — Kali Yuga, the age of fire and destruction — a time when Tantra is lost to the world. It had been prophesied that Tantra would reappear in the age of Kali Yuga to unify the male and female energies. Rediscovering our own inner female power is the only hope this planet has to save itself from its suicidal technology.

Kriya Yoga is a System of Techniques to consciously move energy through the body. There is no belief system, just a path of action which produces results which are powerful, immediate, predictable, repeatable, and objectively verifiable. The techniques work on all levels of a person's life, strengthening the body, calming the emotions, enhancing the thought processes, leading to a balance that can open the door to spiritual awareness. The techniques of Kriya are scientific and practical. It is "action yoga." In this fast paced society we have little time for meditation. Kriya Yoga assists you in maximizing the energies at your disposal so you can get on with the business of living.

Kriya Yoga is one of the most ancient systems on this planet, but it has been revealed only to a select few initiates of mystical orders. The ancient civilizations of India, Egypt, Atlantis — indeed all the developed cultures — practiced some form of Kriya. The American Indians had part of it, as did St. Paul and Jesus. It was lost for a time during the dark ages.

Kriya is the ancient tantric science of rotating consciousness through the astral pathways of the body to produce a profoundly altered state of consciousness. Kriya utilizes a process of "Internal Alchemy" to magnetize the spine, literally pulling etheric energy into the cerebro-spinal fluid and altering its electrical properties. This is the secret of regeneration through "cosmic fire."

The breathing and meditation techniques cleanse and unblock the secret (latent) tunnels between the coccyx (the sacral reservoir of the cerebro-spinal fluid) and cranial cavities. Then the electrically charged fluid (also called Shakti, cosmic fire, or Kundalini) wells up in the unobstructed channels to flood the brain with cosmic energy. This Shakti Kundalini activates the third eye, the seat of individual consciousness, and stimulates the pineal and pituitary glands—direct links to cosmic awareness. It transforms the entire nervous system, so every sense is expanded. It produces a continuous mild orgasm throughout the central nervous system. It brings you to the state of

Samarasa (enlightenment or cosmic consciousness).

From Duality to Unity. In Tantra and other Yogas, there is a science and art of weaving the male and female principles within the human body. Ultimate Reality is One, but we perceive reality as dualistic, that everything has its opposite, and that duality is sexual. We can return to the Oneness only by transcending that duality.

Kriya Yoga is the right-hand path—Dakshina Marga—a rotation of the sexual forces of mind and body with the focus on attaining balance between the male and female aspects of the individual. Practicing alone is an auto-intercourse technique. It is slow and requires diligent effort for many years.

Tantric Kriya Yoga is the left-hand path—Vama Marga—a rotation of conscious sexual forces between two partners, mixing the male and female energies in an internal alchemy. Out of this comes the same illumination that a Kriyaban (celibate Kriya practitioner) can experience, but much more quickly. To connect your energy with your mate's accelerates your progress. It is possible to experience illumination in one ritual!

To balance the male and female energies, you have to be on the earth and in heaven simultaneously. In Maithuna Ritual, you feel very rooted and grounded in the earth, and at the same time you open up into the Nous, the Cosmic Source.

The snake biting its tail is a universal symbol for completion of the earthly experience. When the Kundalini circuit is complete, your karmic obligation has been satisfied and you have no further need for life at the rather primitive level of this planet.

Using Sexual Creative Energy. According to other Yoga systems, practicing sexual union and experiencing orgasm wastes the life-energy, allowing it to return to the earth. The fluids of procreation carry the most condensed, most powerful energy available to us. The "normal" Western sexual experience is totally devoted to throwing that energy out of the body, leaving the lovers drained and exhausted.

The tantric masters knew that when a secret Kundalini pranayam (Cosmic Cobra Breath) is practiced, the life force in the sperm and vaginal secretions could be extracted, retained in the body to vitalize and rejuvenate the system, and projected to the brain to awaken its sleeping potential.

In the sexual ritual (Kundalini Maithuna) you can utilize the sexual secretions of the bodies. By using the tantric breathing and positions you can extract hormone-rich filtrates from the blood by psychic milking of the vaginal dew and semen, pulling their life-producing energies into the cerebro-spinal fluid. Once that energy has been extracted, you don't lose any vital force in orgasm.

Using Orgasmic Energy. The basis of sexual desire and its fleeting fulfillment is the ecstasy of sexual orgasm, the most intense experience anyone can have. In that moment one experiences union with the beloved. There is no separation, no "I" as apart from "you." In that moment we transcend into the state of Samadhi, blissful union between the individual consciousness and the Cosmic. Wave after wave of love and peace infuse waking consciousness. The anxious, striving, separated individual self becomes merged with the total flow of cosmic life energy, bathed in its unchanging quality of intense joy.

The orgasmic experience is available to all, and for many it is the only mystical experience they will ever have. This momentary glimpse leaves us with a deep yearning to repeat it, not just for the sexual release, but for the truth it reveals. Because in that moment we remember who we really are.

In Tantra you can extend the climax to many minutes. Tantra provides a system of techniques for prolonging orgasm in order to experience Unity Consciousness. The state of enlightenment has been described as perpetual orgasm. Once you learn to attain this state in meditation, sex is no longer such a driving need.

In orgasm you are at one with yourself, with your lover, with all creation, with God. There is no time, no past or future, only total presence in the eternal now. The breath stops and the mind is empty. And from this void comes profound love, divine joy and illuminating bliss.

TANTRIC TECHNIQUES

The techniques presented in this book are the essence of Tantric Kriya Yoga. This path uses the following practices:

- **Asanas** - postures to purify the physical vehicle;
- **Pranayama** - breathing techniques to expand consciousness;
- **Dhyana** - meditation to attune yourself to the Divine Current;
- **Mantras** - transcendent sounds which resonate in the body;
- **Yantras** - visual manifestations of mantras;
- **Mudras** - gestures to activate body currents;
- **Bandhas** - energy locks to conserve and move pranic energy;
- **Maithuna** - sexual union.

These practices are complementary and synergistic. Very simple mechanical devices bring energy into the body and move it to where it is needed. We get a minute amount of energy from food. We receive more energy from breathing in the life force (Prana). The most powerful energy is that which comes from sexual intercourse. Doing these exercises will keep your energy at an optimal level — the goal of any Yoga practice.

An important part of this work is building up a psychic reservoir of energy. All Yoga, all systems of personal development, start in the navel center or the solar plexus. You must learn to generate energy at this point for that is how you evolve. This energy starts at the navel and works its way to the top of the head where it activates many dormant brain cells (neurons). This flow of energy to the brain creates an expanded state of consciousness. That is what is really happening in the brain-mind expansion.

That energy reservoir also stimulates the sexual glands. The sexual glands are the key to any higher state of consciousness. If the sexual glands are not strong and functioning at the optimum level, you constantly deplete yourself of energy. The purpose of tantric exercises is to strengthen those glands.

Every movement is to stretch and loosen the spine. When the spinal fluid starts to bubble up, you can actually feel the tingling electrical charge going up and down your spine. You have to make the pelvis loose and flexible so the energy can flow from the sacrum. Tantric exercises contribute to this goal. The spinal cord is where the mystical experience originates.

Tantra's specific, practical techniques put you into a hypersensitive state where every nerve in your body vibrates at a higher frequency, because of increased blood circulation. Everything esoteric can be explained on the physical level. There aren't any mysteries. We take the mystery out of mysticism. This is a technology. These currents open you up to all levels of consciousness. Once you realize the secret of the body, you realize the secret of the universe. Everything is contained within. You are an exact replica of the cosmos. As above, so below.

The techniques presented here are only introductory and prepare the student for more advanced work. But even these beginning practices are extremely powerful. The masters devised these techniques to give you an indication of what you can do without techniques. They are just a starting point, not an end in themselves.

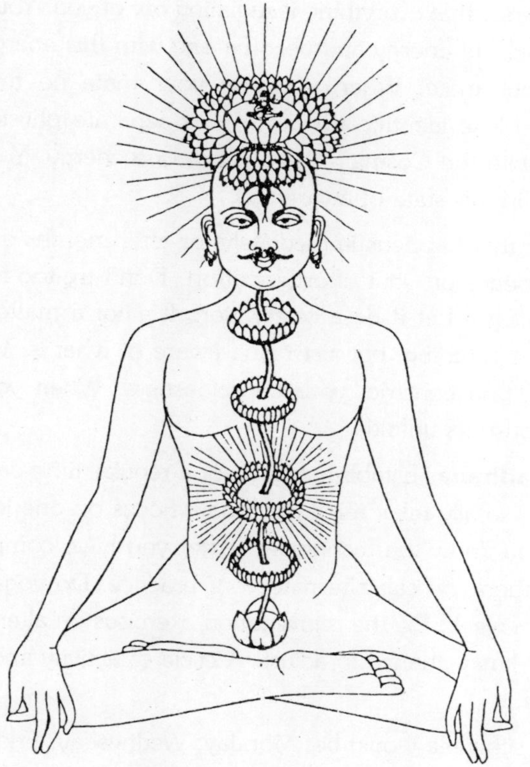

Ultimately all of this practice is preparation for the Cobra Breath. All the Tantra schools, whether from Egypt, China, Persia or wherever, teach the Universal Cosmic Cobra Breath. This sacred technique is the key to Cosmic Awareness. (See Lesson 5)

The Results. Tantric Kriya Yoga can produce results very quickly. You have to be consistent in the practice because you are building a psychic circuit in the body which takes about a week to start forming. We call this process "building the golden body of light." If you and your partner make love twice a day, doing the Cosmic Cobra Breath, you can have the experience of Ultimate Universal Unity in a week.

The purpose of yoga is for you to know that you are the center of your universe, that everything is radiating out of you. You will activate the Kundalini energy and become one with this energy as you join with your mate. When you and your mate do the Breath together, you lose identification with your separate physical selves and merge with the Cosmic. There is just one energy. Your bodies "disappear" in this state of awareness.

Whether that happens immediately, or after months or years of practice, depends on your effortless effort. Don't try too hard. Play with it. Let it go. Let it be a celebration. It's not a matter of concentrating on anything, but just being aware of what is. When you concentrate, you constrict your consciousness. When you let go, your consciousness unfolds.

Your Sadhana. Establish a habit of a regular time each day to go within, to totally relax mind and body. Focus on one lesson at a time until you know the techniques. After you have completed the 12 lessons then you can alternate your practice. Do yoga perhaps three times a week. Do the rejuvenation exercises on alternate days so the body has a chance to adjust. A cycle of activity and rest creates balance.

A good schedule would be: Monday, Wednesday, Friday - Rishi Isometrics; Tuesday and Thursday, Rejuvenation Postures; Saturday, no practice at all; Sunday meditate only; Sexual Activators whenever you're preparing for sexual activity, or any time you want to turn yourself on (which is all the time!).

<u>First</u> do some physical activity to get the circulatory system going, to energize this physical frame. <u>Second</u>, start working at a more subtle level, moving energy through the body. Become aware of everything that is happening inside and around you. <u>Third</u>, sit for meditation. You will have certain experiences, as something happens inside consciousness. Eventually everyone will have those same experiences. The Tantric Kriya tradition is particularly important because it is scientific. Doing certain techniques eventually produces

certain results.

It is important to do what is comfortable for you. There is nothing rigid in your practice. You will learn techniques to turn you on, calm you down, focus your mind, make you dynamic and pull you into the twilight zone. In Tantra we use the mind to beat the mind. We play tricks on it. In some techniques you will find that the thought process shuts off automatically. Using breath, mantra and colors, you soon find consciousness expanding. You can choose the practice that's most appropriate for you at any given moment.

BY-PRODUCTS OF TANTRIC PRACTICE

1. Rejuvenation is one result which is not discussed in most books. Regeneration of your vital organs and revitalization of your sexual glands are most important factors in your spiritual growth. Everyone who practices these techniques finds their aging process slowing down. The results are clearly visible. Take a snapshot of yourself, practice the rejuvenation postures for a week, and then take another snapshot. You will be surprised.

2. Clairvoyance emerges naturally as you begin to stimulate the chakras in the brain. You don't need any psychic training. The Third Eye opens spontaneously.

3. Deepening of Your Relationship. You learn to connect with your mate at all levels. For those whose marriage has deteriorated into the business of managing money and raising children, there is hope for a resurgence of the sexual dynamism that brought you together in the first place.

4. Psychotherapy takes place: release from the phobias, neuroses, resentments, embarrassments, and insults you have suffered, which continue to sap your energy and limit your activity. Expanding consciousness by becoming the Witness is the only therapy that really works.

5. Dream Learning. At night when you go to sleep, you leave your physical body. You travel through many dimensions. One level is the dream state. You don't have to try to get out of your body. It happens automatically. Tension-relaxation, Hong-Sau and the Cobra Breath will take you out of your body but leave you fully conscious of what's happening.

Tantric Kriya Yoga takes you into the state called Bindu — the state between wakefulness and dreaming. You will come to a point where you are asleep physically but wide awake. The quality of your dreams will change, providing a new intensity and meaning. Keep a dream diary to take full advantage of the teaching or cleansing going on in your dreams.

6. Reprogramming Your Subconscious. While it's easy to talk of dissolving the ego, it's far more difficult to do it. The ego is supported by your subconscious mind which is programmed to not be altered. Many well-intentioned teachers urge us to repeat endless affirmations to change our subconscious self-defeating behavior, but affirmations are only the conscious mind talking to itself. We can't reach the subconscious that way.

Hypnosis claims to communicate with the subconscious by inducing a trance state to suspend the conscious mind. The hypnotist tries to limit your sphere of perception until you only hear his voice. His suggestions will have certain effects, but they won't last. The most important limitation is that hypnosis doesn't remove the cause of the problem. Every problem behavior is the solution to another problem. Whatever conflict prompted the compulsion still hasn't been resolved. A hypnotist can suggest that you no longer feel a compulsion to eat, and eating behavior might normalize, but the inner conflict will find another avenue of expression, probably one more subtle, harder to deal with.

Hypnosis-induced trance will take you to the door of meditation. Many so-called meditation techniques are really hypnosis. Only true meditation will allow you to "reprogram" your mental computer, and remove the source of any conflict. Take advantage of the techniques presented here to deal with problems as they come to the surface.

THE TWO SPIRITUAL PATHS

The masters have indicated that there are basically two spiritual paths: the Path of Will and the Path of Surrender. Either you learn self-mastery by great discipline and will power, or by allowing things to be just the way they are, and allowing the cosmic currents to carry you wherever they will. The first path takes amazing self-control, the second takes extraordinary trust. Ultimately, the seeker who has gone as far as he can with discipline will have to surrender. That's the long way around. Alternately, you can just begin with surrender. In many paths there is a guru figure to surrender to. That may be convenient, but it isn't necessary.

We will present two techniques for dealing with subconscious material. You can use whichever is appropriate. For impressing your will upon a wayward subconscious we have Yoga Nidra (Sleep of the Yogi). For observing the subconscious and thereby stripping it of its power, we have Witness Consciousness.

Path of Will. All yogic systems, whether from East India, Tibet, Egypt, or China, start at Manipura Chakra, the Solar Plexus, Cauldron of Fire, the center of personal will. The Bated Breath is a technique that strengthens that will power. When we exhale with a bated breath, using a thrusting motion, we retain the life force and store it at Manipura Chakra. We can accumulate this energy and then take it into the higher centers. We as human beings work basically on the gross level of the physical body. We have to learn to energize the Manipura Chakra to make contact with the Pranic Body, the vital life force body, that surrounds and interpenetrates the physical body. Once we contact that, we can go into the infinite.

Yoga Nidra - Sleep of the Yogi. This technique has been used since time immemorial by Yogis to contact their subconscious minds. It utilizes that moment just as you slip from wakefulness to sleep, Bindu — that moment of transition when both conscious and subconscious minds are available. A suggestion planted at that critical moment, over a period of time, will absolutely manifest.

You can use this technique to bring about changes such as quitting smoking and getting more exercise, but we have introduced it first to bolster you against resistance to doing this work. Resistance is most certainly going to come up. This is a very difficult path, because it requires you to face certain truths you have been hiding from, things about yourself you aren't willing to look at. It takes you into states of mind you've never experienced.

Change is the most stressful thing in life — facing the unknown situation you are not sure how to handle. It takes great courage and trust to give yourself over to the forging of the Cosmic Fire. If you are serious about practicing Tantra, use the Yoga Nidra technique to make a resolution, a commitment to your own growth, to announce to the Cosmos that you are available for instruction, and to attune your subconscious to the imminent changes.

In each lesson you are asked to focus on some aspect of your programming. Use Yoga Nidra to suggest to your subconscious that it is all right to give up its secrets. A good beginning process is presented here. A complete explanation and deeper process is available in our Audio Course, Theta Threshold.

Path of Surrender - Witness Consciousness. When the limited concept you have of yourself, your ego, dedicates itself to the expanded Self, your divine nature, then you have entered the path of surrender. To surrender, you must trust that existence is looking out for your best interests.

The Cosmos is always willing to teach you, and is just waiting for you to be available. In fact it is constantly putting opportunities in your path to learn and to outgrow your current state. You have probably considered them irritations and problems and done everything possible to avoid them.

There is one simple attitude that you need to instill in your being:

The Cosmos gives me exactly what I need.
Whatever comes to me is appropriate
and I will learn from it.

You have gone through your daily life absorbed in the drama - your pleasures and conflicts, your dreams and frustrations. As you mature spiritually you identify more and more with your higher nature and begin to lose interest in the games going on around you. You learn to be in the game and, at the same time, in higher consciousness, watching from a detached persepective.

In Witness Consciousness you totally <u>experience</u> the sensation, thought or feeling going on in the present moment and at the same time <u>observe</u> it objectively, while fully conscious. Then the thought or feeling begins to lose its hold on you and ceases to be a fascination or irritation. Then begins the peeling away of layers of mind-stuff that you have come to think of as part of your self.

Individual Practice

1. Bated Breath is the secret to retaining life force inside the body, to filling yourself up with more prana or vitality.

a) Inhale deeply through the nose. As you exhale produce the whispered sound "SA, SA,...,SA" repeatedly until the air is gone. This is the bated breath. Each sound comes with a little contraction of the diaphragm, bringing the energy all the way down to the navel (Manipura Chakra). Don't force your stomach to go in and out. Just allow a natural thrusting. This gives you a gentle internal massage and wakes up the life force. If you do it properly you can almost hear birds chirping.

b) As you continue the practice you will be able to refine the "SA" sound so it's almost inaudible, so the thrusting becomes more subtle. You can even do it on a mental level as long as you get a micro-movement in the Solar Plexus. This practice will lengthen your life and greatly increase your energy and vitality. That has been proven scientifically.

c) After doing the technique, go through your body. Be aware of any sensations in your body. You will eventually feel a pulse. When you inhale you attract all the negative and positive ions in the air. Those go right into the third eye and automatically create a pulsing sensation. As you exhale with the "SA" sound you will produce a pulsing sensation in Manipura Chakra.

2. Kriya Energization (tension-relaxation) will stimulate the entire body, lighting up like a Christmas tree each energy point (acupuncture point). It cleanses the nadis (energy flows), thus stimulating the Kundalini, thereby expanding your energy field.

Energizing also puts you in the state of balanced awareness, the state of consciousness between sleep and wakefulness, the state where auto-suggestion is most powerful. The entire Yoga Nidra process for auto-suggestion is a long guided meditation. Here is a method you can do now.

A milder version of this process is in the standard repertoire for most stress-reduction experts and hypnotists. Adding the visualization and breath makes this process much more effective.

Part A. To Shock the Muscles and prepare them for deep relaxation and energization. Move in slow motion. Feel the energy flowing through your body.

1) Lie on your back, palms down.
2) Lift your left leg as high as you can and suddenly let it drop.
   Lift your right leg and allow it to drop.
   Lift your left arm and let it drop.
   Lift your right arm and let it drop.
3) Repeat two more times.

Part B. To energize the body and reach Bindu

Consider the body to be divided into 12 parts:

1 left lower leg — 2 right lower leg
3 left upper leg — 4 right upper leg
5 mid section — 6 upper chest
7 neck — 8 left lower arm
9 right lower arm — 10 left upper arm
11 right upper arm — 12 head

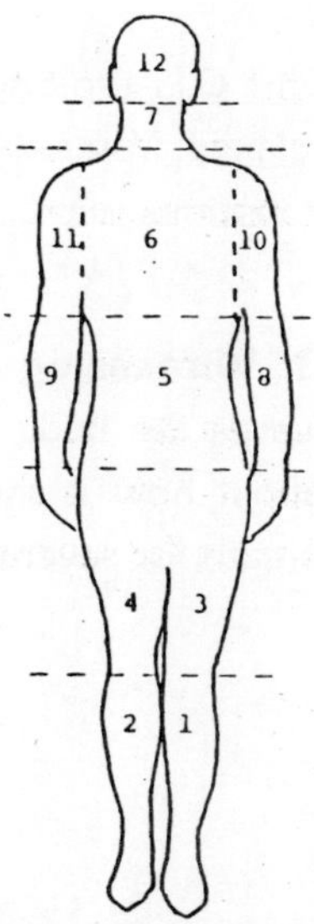

Lie down on your back in a comfortable position with palms up, resting on your thighs. Tense and relax each body part in the order shown above. While tensing, breathe in, and while relaxing breathe out, picturing energy flowing to that body part from the medulla oblongata (at the base of the skull where spinal cord meets brain.) Gaze up at the Third Eye.

When this technique has been mastered, you may combine two symmetrical body parts into a single tension, i.e., tense both the right and left lower legs together.

Set aside a regular time each day to practice, and keep a diary of your experiences.

You can use the tension-relaxation technique for healing yourself. Tense any area that needs healing while inhaling and imagining prana flowing in through the medulla oblongata to that area. Attention should also be focused at the medulla. Relax the area while exhaling, continuing to imagine prana flowing to that spot. This process may be repeated as often as you feel is needed to heal the affected body part.

Part C. Auto-Suggestion At this point mind and body will be very relaxed. You can affirm the resolution you wish to instill in your subconscious mind. It will be open and receptive.

3. Witnessing the Breath. Observe the breath as it enters and leaves the body. Make no attempt to modify it. Have no opinion about how it should be. Give your full attention to watching the breath for several minutes.

Couple Practice

Witnessing Sensory Stimulation

Set aside an hour of uninterrupted privacy. Gather together a wonderful assortment of items with different textures and temperatures — like a feather, a piece of satin, a little ice-water, an egg, some perfume, a variety of music from the gross to the sublime, little tastes of different foods, etc. Let your imagination go. Of course there must be nothing toxic or hurtful.

Invite your partner to lie down on a massage table, bed, or the floor, whatever is comfortable for you both, and gently cover your partner's eyes. Give your partner an experience of the unexpected: a touch, a taste, a whiff, a tone. Let it be a creative adventure for both of you.

At some point reverse positions so each of you has been the giver and the receiver. Usually the man is more comfortable giving than receiving. So let him be the giver first.

As you receive this sensory treat, you will practice Witness Consciousness. Let there be three things clearly distinguished in your mind: 1) The stimulus presented to you; 2) Your body's perception of the stimulus; 3) You watching that perception. You must step back from the experience enough to be a detached observer. You will be saying to yourself something like, "Here I am watching my nose smell this perfume. I am observing my skin responding to the ice water."

Let there be intervals when no stimulus is presented. In those times tune in to sounds in the room, feel the pressure of the spots where your body contacts the floor or bed.

Then look inward for sensations in your muscles, tightness or twitching. Look inward to your organs for any sensations.

Be totally absorbed in your observations. Continue to move back and forth between stimuli from the exterior world and sensations in your interior world. As if you had never noticed before, observe how your nervous system connects you (consciousness) to your body and your environment.

This is a step in learning Witness Consciousness, one of the most important techniques, the ultimate psychotherapy. Once mastered, Witness Consciousness will free you from your past and allow you to live totally in the present.

If you have entered into this exercise with the spirit of play, it just might develop into very sensitive lovemaking. If it doesn't that's also fine. Don't clutter the process with expectations.

Awareness

1. Practice Witness Consciousness while you sit in meditation, or at any time through the day. The more often you practice, the faster your progress will be. Just observe yourself, from a slightly detached position, picking up sensory stimuli from the inner or outer world. Discriminate three separate events — the stimulus, the sensing, the witness.

2. Begin Recording Your Dreams in a journal. They will be filled with messages and healing processes as you do this practice.

3. Use Your Journal to look at various aspects of your life. You will also want to note your breakthrough experiences and insights.

a) Look at your attitudes about sexuality versus spirituality. Of course you consider yourself sexually liberated. Think back to the attitudes impressed on you as a child, whether spoken, or more devastatingly, unspoken. Remember embarrassment about your body and your sexual feelings; confusion about your first period or wet dream; your surprise at learning your parents or the minister had sex; thinking the world might come to an end when you got caught "playing doctor" or some other childhood intimacy that horrified your parents. Those memories are still there, blocking your sexual energy.

b) Look back at all your sexual experiences and partners. How often were you really satisfied, and how often disappointed. Have you harbored thoughts that there is something wrong with you, that you're missing out somehow? Tell the truth!

c) Look for patterns in your relationships: they always abandon you, or you keep control by leaving them first; you always pick a certain type of person, etc. Any factor common to many of your relationships indicates there is something to be learned and you have to keep going through it until you understand it.

d) If you are currently in a relationship, the odds are very strong that one or both of you is dissatisfied, bored, or disappointed with your sexual experience. You're afraid that admiting your dissatisfaction, even to yourself, would destroy your relationship. Or perhaps what you have is wonderful and you don't want to risk change. It is very unusual to find a couple willing to explore the tantric path together, for fear that their relationship would not survive. You must open up communication and assure each other that your love is stronger than your fear.

If you are not in a relationship, and want to be, are you ready to deal with the truth about why there is no one there for you? How you have made that happen? How you can change it when you are ready? (Techniques to draw a perfect partner are taught in advanced training).

Lesson 2

The Breath and Pranic Energy

The Complete Breath. Whether you wish to experience higher consciousness, greater psychic sensitivity, better health - physically and mentally, or full body orgasm, the key is expansion of the breath. Close your eyes for a moment and, without changing anything, just notice your breathing. You will probably observe that it is shallow and fairly rapid. Unfortunately, in this culture, that is normal. The yogis place a great emphasis on learning to breathe slowly and deeply, filling the lungs completely and emptying them completely. You will also notice that the moment you become conscious of your breathing, the breath pattern changes. Conscious breathing is the foundation of breath control.

See how large the lungs are (next page). They have three separate chambers or lobes, but the upper and lower lobes are seldom used. Most people breathe only in the middle lobe. Observe a baby sleeping and you will note that the breath first fills the abdomen and then expands into the chest. This is the natural way to breathe. Most people use less than one seventh of their lung capacity, inhaling one pint of air with each breath. The fully expanded lungs will hold as much as seven pints. When more oxygen enters the system, every cell of every organ is nourished and can perform its task far more effectively. When more oxygen is released to the neurons of the brain, it activates the brain for clearer and more powerful impulses, making the senses more acute and strengthening the entire nervous system. We become much more aware of the subtle energies in and around us.

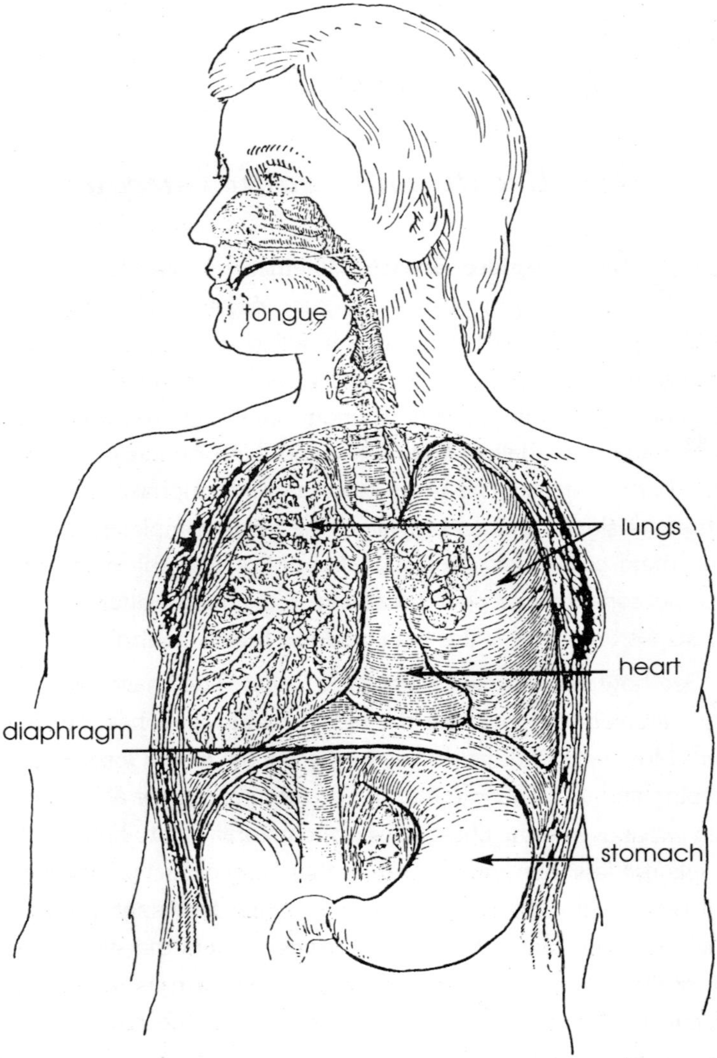

Retaining the inhaled breath for a moment allows extra time for the blood to unload its cargo of waste products and absorb more oxygen. Extra oxygen in the body has remarkable healing and rejuvenation effects. (Hyper-oxygenation techniques can quickly turn grey hair back to its original color).

Exhalation rids the body of carbon dioxide and other waste products of metabolism. When that waste is not thoroughly removed, cells break down and become subject to disease. Unconscious breathing seldom empties the lungs completely.

Access the Unconscious. The nervous system is divided into two parts: the Central Nervous System, for voluntary (conscious) movements, and the Autonomic Nervous System, which automatically regulates body functions (subconscious). Breathing is usually an automatic process, but of all the automatic functions it is the one most easily brought under voluntary control. Thus it is the bridge between the conscious and subconscious workings of our body/mind.

Protect Your Health. The Autonomic Nervous System is further divided into two parts — the sympathetic and parasympathetic. The para-sympathetic system produces a state of relaxation and well-being. The Complete Breath is calming because breathing deeply into the abdomen calls the para-sympathetic nervous system into play. Shallow breathing keeps the sympathetic nervous system in control — the system which prepares you for fight or flight in the face of danger. As far as your body knows, if you breathe shallowly and rapidly you are in danger. The stress of constantly being on alert is a known factor in producing most diseases. Learning to turn off this emergency system and return to a relaxed system is one of the major benefits of the Complete Breath.

Slowing the breath produces dramatic changes in the body/mind. The average person breathes approximately 15 times per minute. When that slows down to eight times per minute the pituitary gland begins to function optimally. That gland regulates all the other glands to ensure the proper balance of hormones, the key to radiant health.

Open Psychic Channels. When you breathe less than four times per minute the pineal gland begins to secrete fully. When the pineal and pituitary glands are stimulated, the third eye begins to function and clairvoyance happens easily.

A Case For Not Breathing. Babies are brought into this world cruelly, with total insensitivity to their feelings. Doctors cut the umbilical cord before the tiny lungs have time to clear the fluid that has filled them in utero, so a baby's first breath is one of panic, taken in searing pain as the delicate tissues are subjected to the rush of air for the first time. Most of us never recover from that trauma, never take a full breath for fear of more pain.

We learned as children that being totally alive was unacceptable to our half-dead parents. Having too much energy created problems. We learned to stifle that aliveness by limiting our breath. We learned at a very early age that when something was too frightening or too painful, we could dull our sensitivity to the moment by holding our breath. It had a numbing effect. It got us through many situations we weren't prepared to deal with. We also learned that when feelings arose which were not acceptable to parents we could switch those feelings off by limiting our breath.

When you are angry you breathe a certain way, and if you don't breathe that way you can't maintain the anger. Conversely, when an actor wants to create a state of anger, he does it by breathing in that particular way. The same principle applies to every feeling. When you are sexually aroused your breathing pattern changes. By stifling that pattern you can turn yourself off. Everyone regulates themselves constantly by their breathing and it's all done unconsciously, automatically.

While this self-regulation has its advantages, has served us well in surviving in this insane world, it also has an unfortunate corollary. True, it has protected us against excessive pain or fear or anger or sexual arousal, but it also has shut down anything that tries to arise in us — too much longing for love, too much pleasure in being close to someone special, too much joy just in being alive. We have settled for a very narrow range of experience, rather than risk the consequences of letting our feelings and awareness flow.

Just as we used breath to suppress feelings, by breathing in certain ways, we can access and bring back into consciousness those dark and hidden parts of the psyche. The feelings didn't go away, but were only buried. Unacknowledged, unexperienced, disowned, they carry on their own life quite beyond our control. Old fears and hurts and resentments left over from childhood still taint our experience indirectly, sabotaging our good intentions. With conscious breathing, these buried feelings begin to surface so they can be dealt with from an adult perspective. We can slowly work through the accumulated feelings, experiencing them, witnessing ourselves experiencing them, and finally releasing them.

At last we become free to experience just what is happening in the moment. Anger comes in, we notice it, experience it, it is gone in the next breath. There is no stockpiling. Breathing deeply through a frightening experience transforms it into a marvelous adventure. You can easily validate this principle in your experience: anxiety plus oxygen equals excitement.

As we become conscious of the moment-to-moment processes of the body, we learn to become aware of the moment-to-moment processes of our thoughts and feelings. Until we make the decision to stay conscious, we will continue to march robot-like through our daily routines and habits, protecting ourselves from anything out of the narrow limits of experience that feel safe. This is sleep-walking. This is the unconscious life.

Why Isn't This Common Knowledge? Why don't the doctors let people know that breathing deeply will make them serene and healthy? The answer is that the process of waking up is frightening The more civilized we are, the more we live in the abstractions of the intellect, the farther removed we are from the feeling states and direct experience of life. Doctors are the most intellectual of all. The process for determining who gets into medical schools assures us of that. They are the least likely to venture into the murky depths of their lifelong accumulation of unfelt feelings.

There are many teachers who come among us to point the way. They typically end up on a cross, drinking hemlock, getting deported, or becoming hermits. The bulk of humanity is not ready to face their own dragon, the guardian of their dark passages. Only a few choose to plunge into the unknown, to work their way through the layer of unfinished experiences, to live at new levels of awareness, to ultimately find themselves.

PRANA AND THE ENERGY BODIES

Prana, the Life Force. The energy which activates the physical body comes through the etheric body in the form of prana, the life-force. This is the component that distinguishes a living being from a corpse. When the prana withdraws, there is no longer life. We ingest a little prana with our food, but primarily it is infused into our bodies as we breathe.

Inhale, Retain, Exhale. Deep breathing, with full and slow inhalation, allows you to extract the most pranic energy possible. The inhalation phase of the breath cycle is the best time to make suggestions to your subconscious mind. That thought is swept along the astral channels with the prana and impressed on the power centers that control your life. The astral flows stop during the retention phase. That is the optimal time to focus the mind. It is said the best meditation happens in the gap between inhaling and exhaling. Exhaling thoroughly expels toxic residue to allow for more infusion of energy. During exhalation you are able to project energy to your lover or for healing someone.

The Physical Body must be mastered at some point in our evolution. It is not separate from, or antagonistic to, the Soul, but simply that aspect of Soul that can be perceived by the senses.

Enlightenment occurs at the physical level, not in abstract space. All the metaphysical processes can be explained in physiological terms - the actions of hormones, metabolism, endorphins, etc. The physical body is the home of the limited conscious mind, governed by the root chakra. Expanded consciousness results when dormant brain cells become activated. You must begin where you are. By bringing consciousness into the physical you get a glimpse of the etheric. Traditionally, the physical body was mastered through Hatha Yoga.

The Etheric (Pranic) Body appears to the psychic eye as a bluish glow around the physical body. Through this pranic sheath, energy animates the physical body. Working with the breath and with Mantra, you can become sensitive to this subtle layer of your being. Governed by the second chakra, this is the home of the unconscious mind, archive of all personal memories. It is contacted in hypnosis because it is so highly suggestible. Physical disease and pain can be created or cured through these suggestions. Emotional traumas that produce our obsessions and self-sabotage can be healed by bringing consciousness to painful memories.

The Mental Body has traditionally been mastered by Raja Yoga. This energy is how we project ourselves into the world.

The Astral Body is the transparent "aura" in which psychics see colors and symbols that represent your emotional state. Once in the Astral Body, you can leave to travel in that plane at will. This is the home of the Collective Unconscious, the Universe's data bank. It is the most subtle of material, at the atomic level. The Astral Body is governed by the heart chakra and can be mastered through devotional Bhakti Yoga.

The first four bodies are on the earth plane. Up to this point movement has been horizontal, from the outside world to the inside. Mastery of the four lower bodies is the full fruition of our human potential, prerequisite to moving into the next plane of existence, from human to super-human, to enlightenment.

The Spiritual (Bliss) Body is the state of full Self Realization, where the Divine Essence is fully embodied. This is the Fifth Dimension that is talked of so much recently.

The Cosmic Body is the state of God-Realization, where Self has totally merged into the All.

The Nirvanic Body is The Void, beyond human comprehension.

MAN MADE GOD IN HIS OWN IMAGE

It has been said that man is made in the image of God. It is our observation that man creates a God to reflect man's self-image. As our consciousness expands we see ourselves in an ever expanding way, and as we advance, our conception of God advances as well.

The untrained mind can deal only with the physical body and the limited five senses. His God looks like a man and behaves like a father who demands obedience and threatens punishment.

After some refinement the senses are able to see, feel, even smell and hear life in the more subtle level, the etheric body. One who is aware of this level can conceive of God as an essence beyond form.

Tantric techniques are all designed to direct that energy toward the spine to stimulate the Kundalini in rising. Once it has risen and you have experienced a glimpse of enlightenment, you can see the divinity in all of creation; there is no longer any need to see the Divine as something separate from yourself.

Individual Practice

1. Shakti Shake.

Start shaking your body. Allow every part to move. If you are total in shaking, the body will take over and you will feel like you are being shaken. Continue at least 5 minutes, as much as 15 minutes. Having the right music helps. Find something which is mostly rhythm. Hawaiian drums are perfect. After you finish, sit quietly and feel the energy buzzing throughout your body.

2. Preparation for the Complete Breath.

To help you master the Complete Breath, we will isolate nine areas of the lungs and concentrate on expanding one area at a time. Sit in a high back chair or on the floor against a wall. You could sit back to back with a partner. Breathe through the nose, three times in each area.

Part A. Lower Lobe

1) When the lower part of the lungs expands, the abdomen must distend to make room, (even through you may feel that is not attractive). Place your hands on the abdomen and, as you inhale, expand the abdomen, feeling it press against your hands. As you exhale, draw the abdomen back in.
2) Now the hands go on the sides at the waist, as you again inhale and expand, focusing on the area under your hands. Exhale and feel the sides return to normal.
3) To monitor expansion in the back part of the lower body, inhale and feel your back pressing against the chair or wall. Exhale and feel it pull away.
4) In a single breath, combine the three previous exercises. As you slowly inhale, expand the front, sides and back of your lower torso. Hold the expansion. Exhale and feel the body contract.

Part B. Middle Lobe

1) Place your hands over your lower ribs in front. As the chest expands feel the hands moving out. Exhale and focus on the chest returning to normal.
2) Place your hands on the sides of your chest. Focus on the sides as they expand and contract with the breath.
3) Feel your back against the chair as you breathe and expand the center back.
4) In a single breath, expand the front, sides and back of the center chest. Hold the expansion. Exhale and feel the body contract.

Part C. Upper Lobe

1) Place your hands at your collarbone. Inhale and expand, lifting the shoulders to earlobe level, exhale and return.
2) Tuck back of hands into armpits and inhale/expand, again lifting shoulders. Exhale/return.
3) Feel your shoulders increasing in pressure against the wall or chair as you inhale. Hold. Exhale and feel the pressure decrease.
4) In a single breath expand the upper lungs—front, side and back —while lifting the shoulders. Hold a moment and relax.

Practice this preparatory technique until you feel comfortable and natural in a full expansion. At that time you are ready to go on to the Complete Breath.

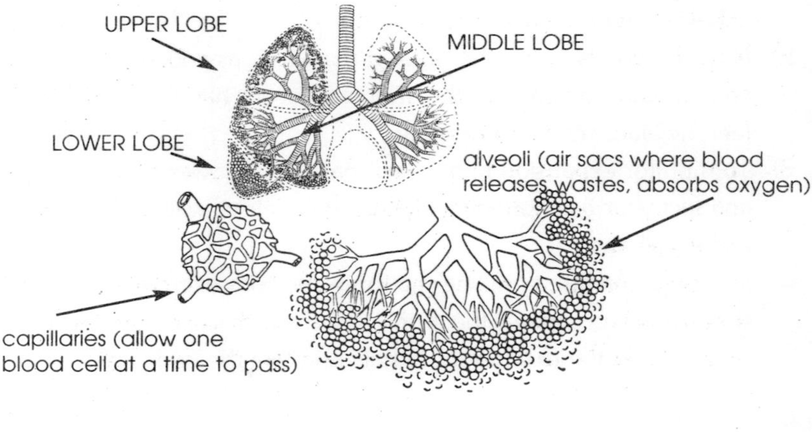

3. Complete Breath Technique.

Sit in a meditative posture (cross-legged or lotus) or in a chair. Close your eyes and maintain focus on the sacrum. Feel how it moves and heats up as you breathe. Be aware of the connection between the sacrum and the third eye.

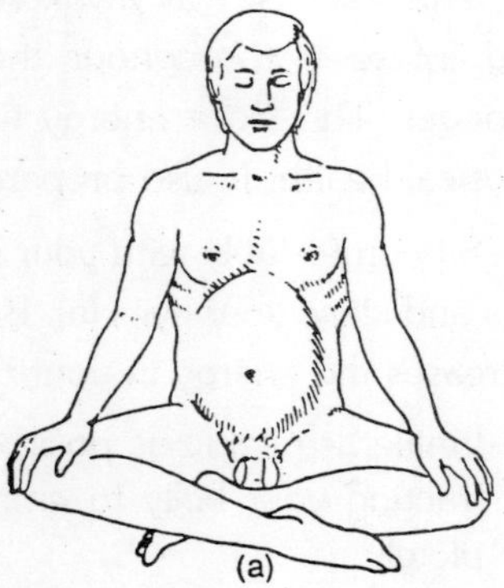

(a)

1) Inhale through the nose, about 3/4 full, expanding the belly (a) and then the chest (b) like inflating a balloon. Pull your shoulders up and forward to fill top of lungs (c).
2) Tense every muscle,including the buttocks. Hold as long as is comfortable
3) Inhale a sniff of air. This relieves the tension and makes it easier to exhale slowly.
4) Exhale through the mouth. Relax the shoulders, tighten the belly. Rock gently back and forth on the sacrum massaging the base chakra.

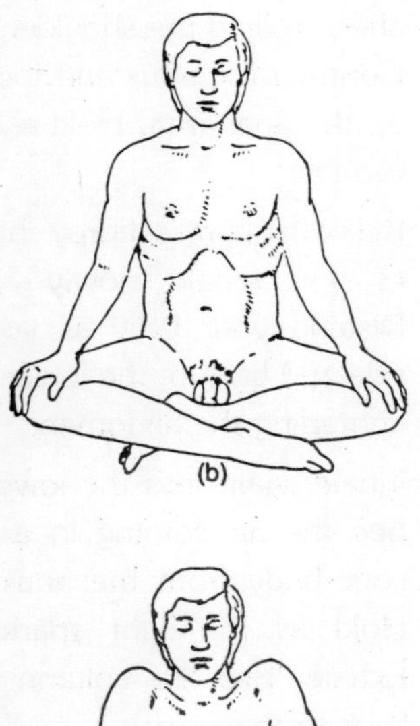

(b)

Repeat the pranayam 7-9 times.

CAUTION: Don't strain the lungs. Slowly increase the amount of time for each breath. If you have high blood pressure, don't hold your breath.

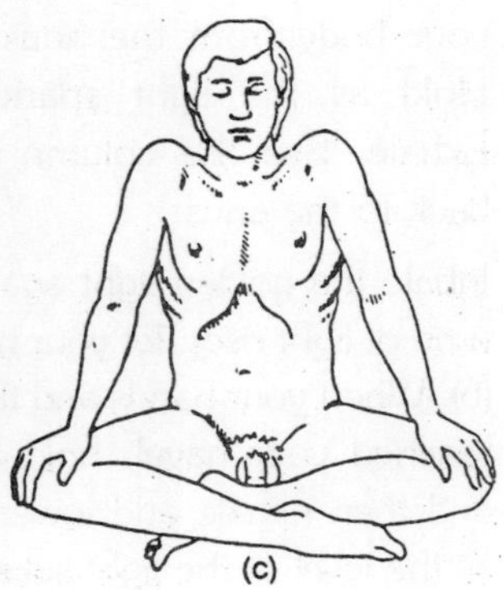

(c)

4. Prana Mudra.

This exercise will awaken the dormant life energy (prana shakti) and infuse it throughout the body. You will feel more alive and stronger. The extra energy will boost your personal magnetism and physical health. It also prepares you for deep meditation.

Sit comfortably with your spine straight. Place your hands on your legs and close your eyes (a). Breathe in and out through the nose. This increases the energy in your body.

1) Inhale as deeply as possible, then exhale contracting your belly to empty your lungs completely.
2) Without inhaling, press your chin onto your chest, rolling the shoulders up and forward. Contract the anus and focus your attention on the anal area. Hold as long as is comfortable.
3) Relax the contractions, chin and anus, as you inhale slowly and deeply. Distend your belly as you fill front, side and back of the lower torso. Hold a moment and then exhale, tightening the abdomen.

(a)

4) Inhale again into the lower part of your torso. See the air coming in as golden light, filling your body from the anus up to your navel. Hold as the light sparkles and dances. Exhale. See the column of light recede back to the anus.
5) Inhale the golden light again. As the column of light rises, let your hands be lifted up (b). When your hands and the light have reached your navel, hold a moment, and then exhale and lower the hands as the level of the light subsides.

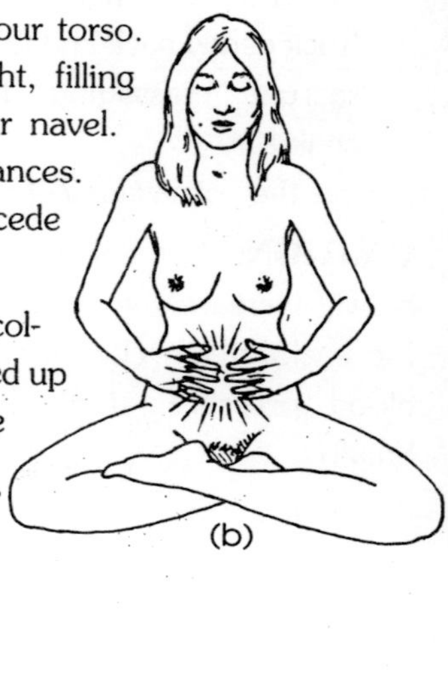

(b)

6) Repeat steps 1-5, this time allowing the breath, the column of light, and then your hands, to rise to the middle of your chest.
7) Repeat steps 1-5 again, this time with the breath/column/hands rising up to your throat as you raise your shoulders.
8) Finally, inhale and feel the energy column and the hands raise to the navel, to the heart, to the throat. As the light spreads like a wave into your head, spread your arms out to the side (c). Visualize light radiating from your head, from your whole being, radiating peace to all mankind. Hold as long as is comfortable.
9) Return slowly to the starting position, with your hands floating at the level of the light column as it recedes to the throat, heart, navel, anus.
10) Relax as you breathe normally. Notice how your body feels. You have experienced yourself as a being of light. This is your true nature. You have come home.

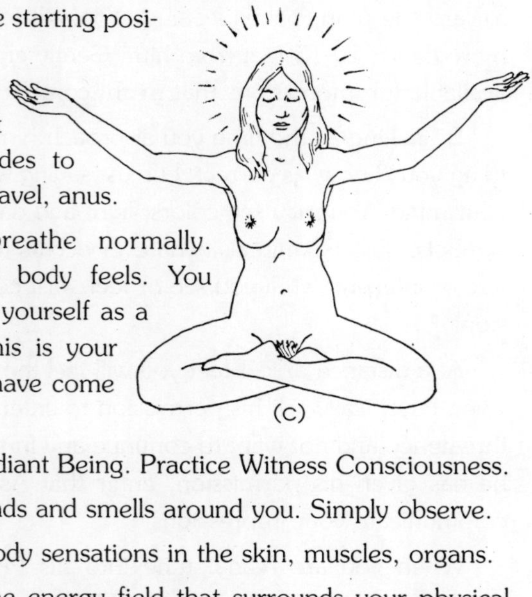
(c)

11) Sit quietly as a Radiant Being. Practice Witness Consciousness.
    a) Notice the sounds and smells around you. Simply observe.
    b) Witness your body sensations in the skin, muscles, organs.
    c) Be aware of the energy field that surrounds your physical body.
    d) Turn your focus inward and watch your thoughts as they drift by. Don't have an opinion about them. Make no effort to change them. Only watch.

Couple Practice

1. Prana Mudra can be done with a partner. As your arms are extended and light radiates, send that light to each other. Let your partner experience you as a being of light. Share your energy.

2. Energy Body Reading. While you are both still in a highly sensitized state, become acquainted with each other's energy bodies. Move to opposite corners of the room. Let the woman slowly walk toward the man, palms leading. You will feel the air become a bit more dense 10-15 feet from him. Gently enter his mental body. Be available for impressions that might come to you.

Be talking all the time you approach him, not waiting for something you "know" is correct, but just saying whatever comes through your mind. You may see colors, light and dark patches around him, symbols, objects, animals, whatever occurs to you. Don't try to analyze or interpret what you see or feel. Just communicate the impressions.

At a distance of 2-4 feet you will feel the edge of an even denser layer. Psychically ask his permission to enter his space. He may feel threatened and not want to continue any further. When you feel that he has given his permission, enter that Astral Body. Continue to communicate your impressions.

When you are ready, tune into his Pranic Body. Place your hands 2-3 inches from his body. Hold your receiving hand in front of the chakras at his genitals, navel, heart, throat and forehead. At each point, notice the different texture of the energy. Some places may be hot, others cold. Some may feel soft, others piercing. Tell him what you perceive and then let him respond.

Reverse roles and let the man now "read" the woman. It may not come as easily to him, as it is not his normal mode of gathering information. He should not compare his "performance" to hers.

Enjoy whatever comes through and communicate it. Let your intuitive side get a little exercise. You have nothing to lose.

3. Complete Breath to Delay Orgasm. Make love at this point. You might be pleasantly surprised at the level of intimacy that is possible. When you feel that orgasm is close, perform the Complete Breath to pull up the energy through your body. This will delay your climax and allow you to build to a higher level. When you do climax it will be more intense.

Be aware of how rapid breathing promotes excitement and muscle tension, and how slow breathing promotes a deeper joy and relaxation. See what your breathing patterns have been while making love.

Awareness

1. Become Aware of Your Breath Patterns in various situations Observe when you breathe shallowly, when you hold your breath entirely. See what you do when you are afraid. (Go ride on a roller coaster or watch a horror movie). Notice your reaction to anger or irritation (waiting in line, inconsiderate drivers). What is your usual pattern when absorbed at work? What happens when you watch T.V?

2. Each Time You Become Aware of Holding, take a Complete Breath and fill yourself with light and consciousness. See how the world around you is transformed. It has been said if you would stay aware of every breath for one full day, you would become enlightened.

3. When Someone Irritates You it is probably because:

a) You see in him a part of yourself that you don't like. You refuse to see that quality in yourself and don't like to see it in someone else;

b) The way he mistreats you mirrors the way you mistreat yourself;

c) He reminds you of some grievance you are attached to — someone you haven't forgiven, some limitation you haven't made peace with;

d) He won't allow you to twist the truth the way you usually do, won't fall for your games, won't support your favorite delusions, won't ignore the obvious.

Any disturbing situation can be turned to your advantage or wasted. You can either look inward to see what buried fear or hurt or anger has been reactivated and bring it to surface, or you can look outward and blame someone for misusing you. Either you learn and grow from the situation or you miss the opportunity. Then the cosmos has to go to the trouble of setting the situation up again and again until you finally see it. When you realize that someone is causing you distress, be grateful to that person for he is your teacher. By being exactly the way he is, he has "pushed a button" in your subconscious. Now that "button" can become conscious and you are one step closer to freedom.

Lesson 3

Asanas: Charging the Body with Pranic Energy

Most Americans associate the word "yoga" with the complex postures they see on TV. The postures come out of a very ancient tradition. They were designed to prepare the body for long periods of sense withdrawal and marathon meditation. The methods were developed for bodies in ancient India, which were quite different in their vibratory patterns from bodies in our modern western world. Even if these practices were appropriate for our body energies, there aren't many of us trying to meditate for 3-4 hours a day.

Indians always sit in a squat, even to eat their meals. They are prepared to sit comfortably in a lotus position. A Western body must stretch out those muscles. Mastering the postures is a long and tedious process, requiring the supervision of a good teacher and more discipline than most of us have. Some people are simply too stiff to ever assume the postures.

In Tantra you don't have to sit in the lotus position. You can sit in whatever position is comfortable as long as your spine is straight. Don't feel that you can't do yoga if you can't do these strange postures. It's not necessary.

A steady routine of Hatha Yoga makes you too passive. You need to balance with something more dynamic. We live in a dynamic world and need a spiritual path to match. Those who think they will save the world by sitting in meditation are fooling themselves. It takes action and energy and youth.

Hatha Yoga has traditionally been the means by which yogis mastered the gross physical body. A more advanced system of Hatha is practiced by the Rishis, holy men high in the Himalayas.

These simple movements, which almost anyone can do, will provide the main health benefit of Hatha Yoga - stretching and loosening the spine - but are more efficient and dynamic. The spinal cord is the point of origin for all transcendent experiences. When you begin to awaken Kundalini, you will feel the tingling sensation of energy going up and down the spine.

It is Kundalini energy which stimulates the endocrine glands. Their increased performance rejuvenates and revitalizes the physical body. One of the by-products of Tantra is its ability to slow down the aging process, which is governed by the endocrine glands. If you're on the right path, your daily practice includes something to stimulate the endocrine system. These asanas also strengthen the five main organs that maintain our life.

Rishi Isometrics are a system of postures that are more geared to the American life-style. They have a marvelous effect on the neck and shoulders. For those who spend most of their working lives at a desk, stiffness of the shoulder muscles is a chronic condition. Energy cannot flow through tense muscles. You must learn to bring those tensions to rest. There are in each of us muscle tensions which never relax; muscles which have been contracted for so many years we have long forgotten how it felt to relax. When the tensions finally let go, you get a startling rush of energy.

The Rishi Isometrics use the principle of dynamic tension to energize the body. Rather than relaxing into a position as in Hatha Yoga, you work one muscle against another isometrically. When muscles are tense, the flow of blood is restricted. When this tension is relaxed, (coordinated with inhalation) the muscle receives a sudden rush of oxygen-rich blood, loaded with prana (life force). This gives us a sense of flowing, of total bliss. Tantric Kriya Yoga is union through action. You are creating energy by going into a deeply relaxed state.

These movements are particularly beneficial in removing waste products in the lymph system. Any movement of muscles squeezes these vessels, pushing the material toward the heart for removal. This set of exercises focuses on those areas in the body where lymph nodes are most numerous: the throat, underarms, and the groin. It wrings out the static contents of the nodes.

We teach these physical exercises to prepare the body for the initiation and for Tantric lovemaking. We prepare our bodies to have stamina when we go into a sexual encounter. A neglected or toxic body cannot contain the powerful higher energies. The body is best prepared by doing internal exercises. Aerobics and weight lifting have some value, but can be dangerous. They are too strenuous and put stress on the body which simply isn't necessary. You can get more energy flow by doing very gentle movements.

When Westerners work on their physical bodies, they are primarily concerned with the external form: muscle definition, fat distribution, physical strength. They work out mechanically, with their minds on something else. When Yogis do physical practices, it is with the intention of bringing consciousness inside the body, becoming sensitive to every bodily function, being offended by any toxicity or obstruction and working to purify every organ and system to allow it to function optimally.

As you master the physical body, you must move from the external awareness to an internal awareness. From that point, it is an easy step to becoming aware of the etheric body, of the subtle energy flows that animate the physical dimension. The movements cleanse the etheric body, stimulating certain nadis (energy paths) and sub-chakras.

Individual Practice

1. Rishi Isometrics.

Use these asanas before meditation to relax, stimulate and prepare the body. Be totally present, conscious of each breath, your mind focused on the movement and the energy produced. Move slowly and gracefully. Perform each part at least three times, as many as seven. Always inhale through the nose and exhale through the mouth. NOTE: If you have heart problems or high blood pressure, build up to this movement very gradually.

Part A. Stretching Up

1) To open the front of the lungs: As you inhale (nose), sweep the arms to the sides and then overhead. Stretch up, lifting onto your toes. Elongate the spine. Press the palms together to create dynamic tension in the arms and underarms (Eventually learn to tighten every muscle in the body with the 12-body-part tension.) Hold the breath, hold the tension for a few seconds. As you exhale (mouth), lower the arms. Relax and feel the streaming sensations in your arms and shoulders. Repeat twice or more.

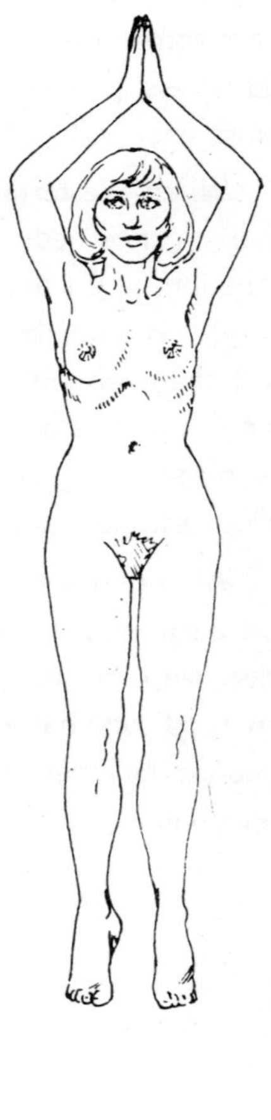

2) To open the back of the lungs: Inhale, stretch up as before, this time pressing the back of the hands together overhead. Feel tension in the shoulders. Inhale up, press and hold, exhale and relax. Repeat.

Part B. Side Bend

1) Stretch left side: Stand with feet shoulder width apart. Inhaling, stretch arms overhead and lock the thumbs, pulling one thumb against the other to create dynamic tension. Exhaling (mouth), bend slowly to the right side, keeping the elbows in line with the ears. Drop the head to the side. Feel the line of tension from the side of your foot to the tips of your fingers. Hold the breath out, hold the tension, for a few seconds. As you inhale (nose), return to upright position, arms overhead, holding tension.

Repeat twice or more.

Relax arms to sides. Focus on the energy movement.

2) Stretch right side: Raise arms overhead, reversing the thumbs. Pull to create tension and bend slowly to the left. Continue as above.

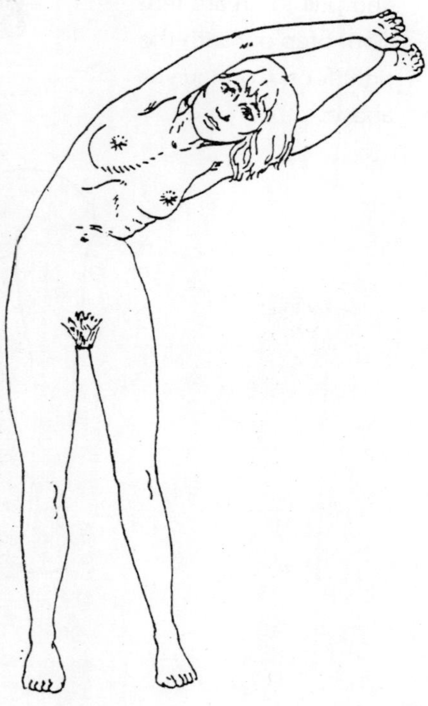

Part C. Forward Bend

1) Clasp thumbs behind your back, pulling one thumb against the other. Step out with your left foot. On the exhale (mouth), bend forward, lifting the arms as high as possible. Lift the chin to feel tension in the throat. Feel tension in the groin. Bend the knee if necessary. Feel the pull from sacrum to medulla.

Hold the tension for a few seconds. As you inhale (nose), return to upright posture, thumbs still clasped, relaxing tension. Repeat twice more. Then return arms to sides, feet together, relax completely.

2) Switch the thumbs and pull to create tension. Step out with the right foot. Continue as above.

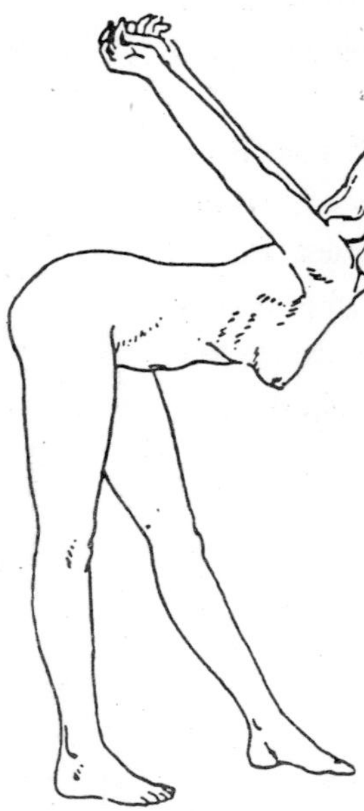

Part D. Back Bend

1) Feet together. On the inhale, press your palms together in front and raise the arms overhead. Holding the breath, lean back, drop the head back, arching the back as much as possible, with tension in the arms. Tense the entire body and focus on the sacrum. Hold the breath, hold the tension.

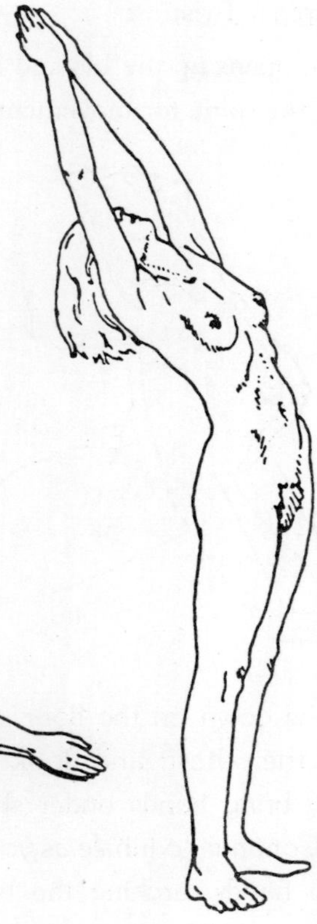

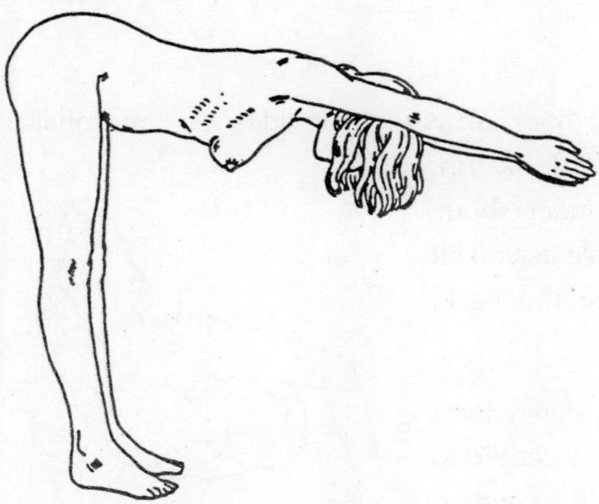

2) Exhale (mouth) as you return to an upright position, relaxing tensions, arms still extended overhead. Bend forward until torso and arms are parallel to the earth. Stretch the arms, stretch the spine. You will feel the energy shoot up your spine. Repeat twice more.

3) After the last exhale, drop the arms and slowly come to upright.

Part E. Spinal Twist

This asana opens up the Ida and Pingala channels (female and male) preparing the spine for movement of Kundalini through Sushumna.

1) Lie face down on the floor, arms to your sides. As you inhale raise the chest and look up. Slowly bring hands under shoulders. Continue to inhale as you lift up on hands, arching the back, looking at ceiling.

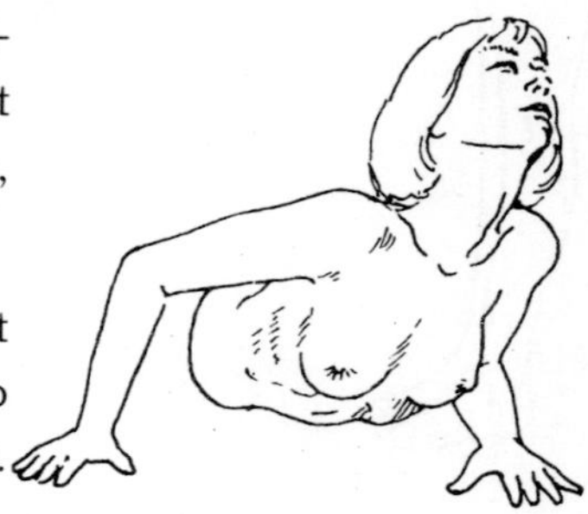

2) Retaining the breath, slowly twist to the right side, back to center, to the left side, back again to center.

3) On the exhale slowly return to prone position, arms at your sides. Repeat.

4) Roll over into the Corpse Pose and totally relax for a few minutes.

2. The Cleansing Breath.

Those who live in an air polluted environment, those who smoke, or used to smoke, or share space with smokers (Did we miss anyone?) have an accumulation of debris in their lungs. Remember the lungs don't have an exit. Whatever goes in your mouth can eventually find its way out, but that's not true for the lungs. Our intention is to bring more prana into the body. To do that the lungs must be cleaned out to operate at maximum efficiency.

The Cleansing Breath releases those accumulated toxins, along with toxins newly formed each time you move your body. After doing the asanas, perform the Cleansing Breath 7 times.

1) Sit on your heels with your hands on your thighs. Inhale deeply through the nose and retain the air for 6 counts.
2) Begin bending forward as you release part of the air through your nose with a forceful snap of the diaphragm. Continue with 3 or 4 more such expulsions.

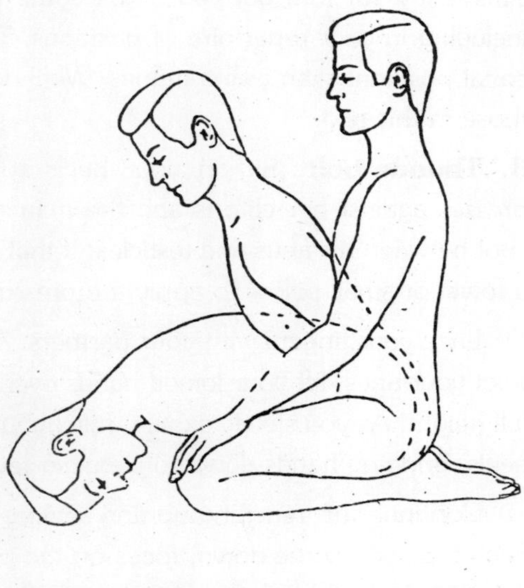

3) When the air seems to be expelled and your head is touching the floor, continue to snap the diaphragm until you know there is nothing more to release. Press your fingers into the solar plexus to force out the last of the air.
4) Slowly raise to an upright position as you draw in another breath.

Couple Practice

1. The Rishi Isometrics given above can be done with a partner. Simply maintain eye contact through the exercises. When you stop to experience the energy flooding through your body, be aware of the energy in your partner's body as well.

2. Asanas as Sexual Positions. Yoga emerged out of Tantra. Many yoga asanas are really sexual positions. Get out your book of yoga postures and see how many of them will work as sexual positions. Get a book of erotic Indian Art - Kama Sutra or something similar. Look at the positions of the couples, the wilder the better. This is just for fun, but you might come up with something worth including in your repertoire of positions. There really are dozens of coital positions with asana names. We'll not concern ourselves with those in this text.

3. Thunderbolt. Sit on your heels so that the woman's heel presses against her clitoris and the man's heel presses against the spot between his anus and testicles. If that's not comfortable, roll up a towel or small pillow to apply the pressure at that spot.

Lace your fingers with your partners. As you slowly inhale, contract your anus, lift your joined hands overhead and raise up to your full height. As you slowly exhale, relax your anus, sit back onto your heels, bringing hands down to shoulder level.

Continue this reaching up and settling back for 3 to 5 minutes. Each time you come down, focus on the pressure against your genitals. At the end hold each other and allow your bodies to relax to the floor. Lie in each other's arms and feel the energy moving.

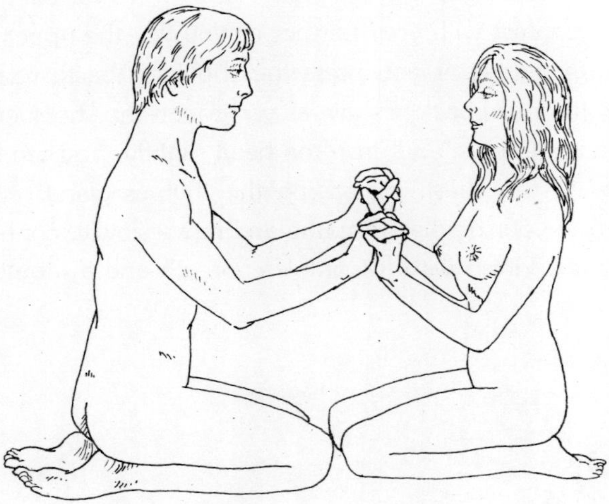

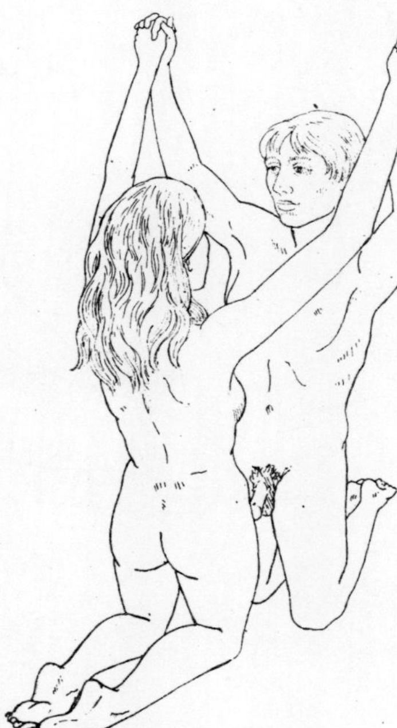

4. Anahata Massage. Sit on your heels or towel as before. Maintain eye contact with your partner as you flex the upper spine back and forth. Inhale as you press the shoulders back, relax the anus and tilt the head back. Exhale as you round the shoulders forward, contract the anus, and drop the head slightly. You are opening and closing the chest, massaging the thymus gland. As you move, stimulate your nipples. Breathe and move slowly, continuing for 3-5 minutes. Finish with a Complete Breath and a moment to enjoy the energy.

5. Third Eye Attunement. Lie on your sides, foreheads touching. Match your breathing so one is breathing out as the other breathes in. Concentrate on sending energy back and forth, sending on the exhale, receiving on the inhale. Continue for 3-5 minutes.

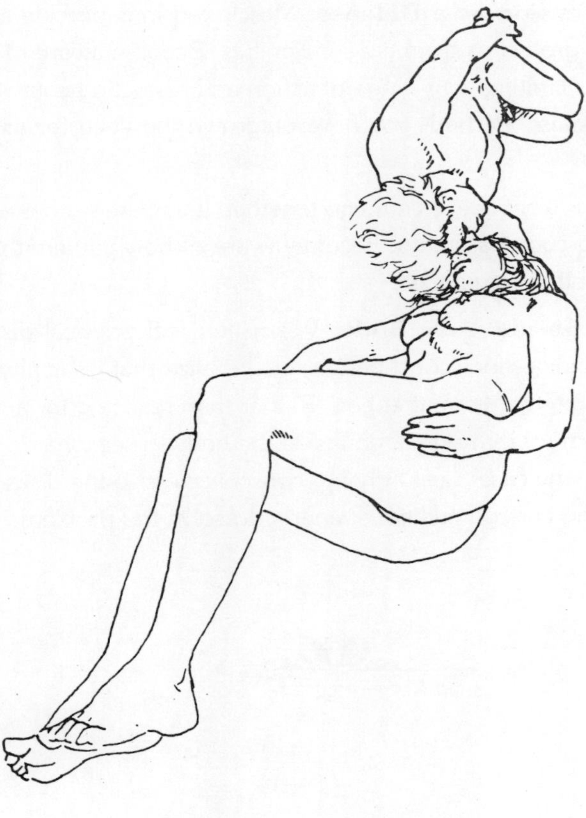

Awareness

1. Becoming Aware of Muscle Tensions. As you go through your daily activities, notice the tensions, particularly in your shoulders and neck. Do a Rishi Isometric stretch with a deep breath every time you become aware of stiffness. Get used to the experience of functioning without tension. Remember these exercises are not isolated from your life. Every moment could be lived meditatively if there were no tensions to block the energy.

2. Using Tension as a Defense. Muscle tensions provide a sort of armor to protect us from life's indignities. Become aware of how that armor is limiting your range of action and restricting your range of consciousness. Perhaps you have outgrown the need for all that protection.

Tension is what keeps your ego together. If you are serious about transcending ego, it's time to become aware of how you limit yourself by holding your muscles.

3. Getting Inside Your Body. When you feel physical distress (headache, indigestion, constipation, etc.) realize that your physical body is trying to get your attention. Rather than reaching for a medication to turn off that signal, go inside the body to see what is happening. In many cases, just bringing consciousness to the distressed area will bring enough additional energy to solve the problem.

Lesson 4

Cosmic Unity of Opposites

We live in a world of duality. The structure of every life form, the processes of mind and body, all have their male and female aspects, opposite and complementary. This is the Divine Play—the parts dance with each other and act out the drama of incompleteness seeking completion. This polarity sets up a tremendous cosmic force. But duality is the source of all suffering, as the sense of incompleteness is very painful. Tantra is the interweaving of the male and female, the positive and negative energies, to return to the cosmic unity vibrating as one.

Hindu mythology personifies the male aspect as Shiva, dwelling above the crown of the head and the female aspect as Shakti, sleeping at the base of the spine, symbolized by a serpent, Kundalini. Through great effort Shakti must awaken and make the arduous journey up the spine. When finally she is reunited with Shiva, they live forever in transcendent bliss. Only through woman can man come to enlightenment, as she is the dynamic principle. Thus in Tantra, female energy (symbolized by Divine Mother) is worshipped. (As in all mythology, these stories and deities only symbolize aspects of human nature and aren't to be taken literally.)

Our culture worships male energy. The computer technology, the breakdown of home life, the increasingly abstract technical professions, pollution of the earth, all display the dominance of male principles and contempt for female principles. Women struggling for recognition have simply acted more male, abandoning the power of their female energy. This has only made things worse. This culture is sick because the energies are badly out of balance. High power technology without reverence for life is very dangerous. The tantric point of view is desperately needed.

Duality in Relationships. Each individual is a mixture of masculine and feminine traits. In our sexual relationships we seek completeness by choosing partners who complement our own energy. We can learn from our partner how to manifest our own latent aspects. Some couples after many years of marriage look and act alike. They have taken on each other's characteristics and met in a middle ground between the polar extremes.

MASCULINE	—	FEMININE
Shiva / Cosmic Father	—	Shakti / Cosmic Mother
Lingam /External genitals	—	Yoni / Internal genitals
Projecting	—	Receptive
Cosmic consciousness	—	Cosmic energy
Universal soul	—	Individual soul
Spirit	—	Nature
Positive	—	Negative
Active	—	Passive
Solar / Warming	—	Lunar / Cooling
Right nostril / Pingala	—	Left nostril / Ida
Left brain hemisphere	—	Right brain hemisphere
Sympathetic N. S.	—	Para-sympathetic N. S.
Electrical	—	Magnetic
Acidic	—	Alkaline
Discharges energy	—	Retains energy
Prefers raw sex	—	Prefers cuddly sensuality
Rational / Logical	—	Intuitive / Emotional
Linear / Detailed	—	Holistic / Diffuse
Abstract/Lost in thought	—	Practical / Down to earth
Needs adventure	—	Geared for survival
Gives love to get sex	—	Gives sex to get love
Objectifies sex partner	—	Personalizes sex partner

It's not easy to shift into your dormant side. Some couples are highly polarized and seem stuck because one, or both, is unwilling to give up their role.

One of our students, a beautifully groomed lady in her sixties, grew restless at the end of each class. It seemed her husband of many years didn't allow her to be out after 10 p.m. Even that was a concession she'd struggled long to get, for this controlling fellow wanted her at home, available to him, and looking beautiful all the time.

This had been fine with her when they first forged their unwritten contract decades before. Then she was comfortable being totally passive and letting him take care of everything. But she had matured and was now ready to assume a more active role. He was not willing to allow her that space. To protect the relationship she could not explore her limits. He was unwilling to share her experimentation with new thoughts and ideas. Both were stuck.

To say that men are one way and women are another way is simplistic. We can define the polarities of masculine and feminine qualities, and observe that most women display predominately feminine characteristics and most men display masculine traits. However, many people in female bodies display very masculine qualities, rejecting any femininity, and many in male bodies express great femininity, rejecting their masculine energies. Actually, in many relationships the woman is the masculine force, and the man more feminine. Between them there is a balance.

Finding a Balance and Union Between Your Own Internal Shiva and Shakti is your ultimate task. Some therapists encourage women to become more feminine and men, more masculine, assuming that increasing the polarity will improve a relationship. The tantric approach is to expand, not to become more polarized. Either male or female energy by itself is pathological. We must attain an internal balance. Only when we have mastered both energies, and manifest them comfortably, can we be appropriate to the moment. In an emotional moment you are there to feel it. In an intellectual exchange you are there to understand it. Being balanced doesn't exclude the extremes. It only increases the size of your playing field. Only when we have realized our inner completeness do we find our divinity.

THE DUALITY OF ETHERIC ANATOMY

The Nadis. "Nadi" is the Sanskrit word for "astral energy flow." The nadis form a network of 72,000 circuits that carry subtle electrical currents (prana) through the pranic body to all parts of the physical body, keeping the cells healthy and vital. They correspond to the meridian system, and are related to the nervous system.

When a part of the body twitches, that indicates that the energy flow had been blocked, and is releasing, affecting the nerves. This is called a Kriya. One of the first steps in Yoga is to unblock the nadis so that energy runs through them freely. This is accomplished by the Isometrics and Nadi Kriya techniques (see Lesson 5).

The Three Main Nadis are called Ida, Pingala and Sushumna. Ida carries female energy up the left side of the spine and Pingala carries male energy down the right side of the spine with connections to each energy center along the spine.

Ida and Pingala are symbolized by the intertwined snakes of the Caduceus. The two channels begin at the perineum (between anus and genitals) and meet again at the base of the nose. Sushumna, the central channel, follows the spine itself and carries the Kundalini. Only when the male and female energies are exactly balanced can the prana spill into Sushumna to be carried upward to the brain. This is what is meant by Kundalini rising.

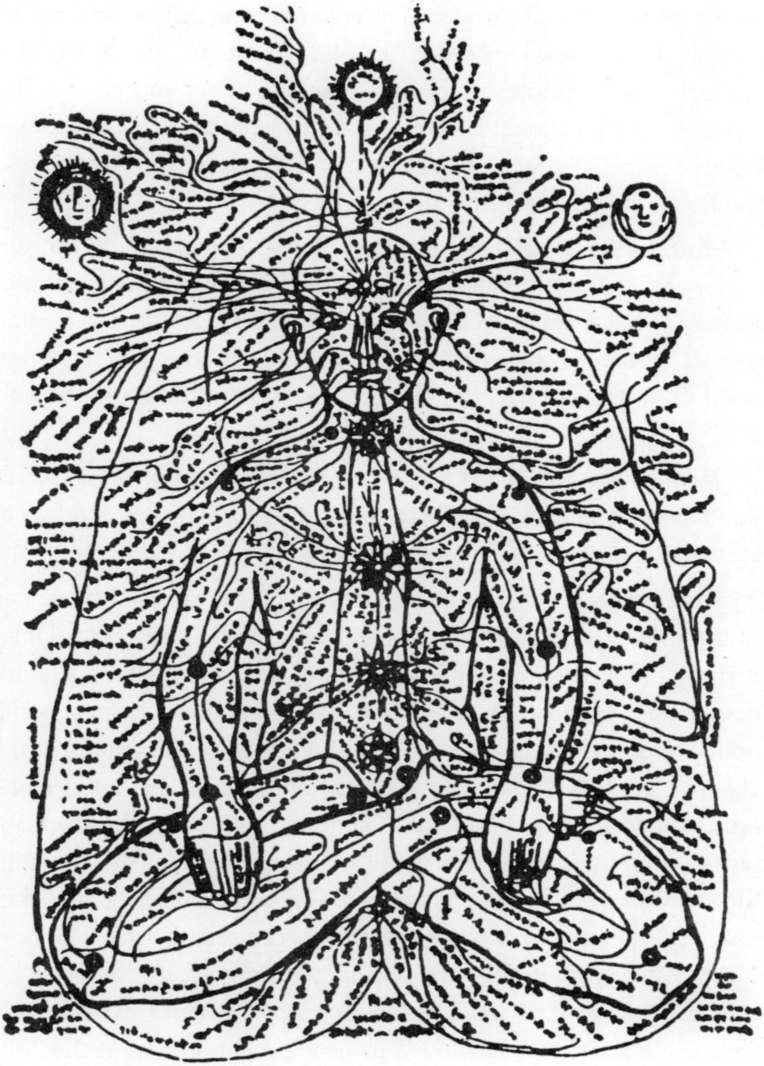

Ancient diagram of the Nadi Currents and chakras. The names are in Sanskrit.

Ida is activated by the left nostril. A negative charge is imparted to the prana inhaled through that nostril by the cilia which line the nostril. This energy is called feminine or lunar. Breathing only through Ida promotes a receptive and cooling mood, soft but dynamic, compassionate energy. It stimulates the astral (emotional) body. This is the energy of the earth and it governs the lower half of the body, the back and the left side.

Pingala is activated by the right nostril. The cilia in that nostril impart a positive charge, called masculine. Breathing only through Pingala invokes clarity and creative vision. It stimulates the abstract Mental Body. This is the energy of the sun bringing light and warmth. It governs the top half of the body, the front and the right side.

People who are in the habit of breathing through their mouth don't get the negative/positive pranic energy and they tend to be lethargic and sickly.

Sushumna is the nadi that goes through the central hollow part of the spinal column, the tube which carries the cerebro-spinal fluid. It starts at the reservoir of spinal fluid at the base of the spine and goes up to the medulla oblongata, and then through the psychic bridge to the center of the skull (Cave of Brahma) and out the crown chakra. The Sushumna is activated when both the Ida and Pingala are open. You must learn how to charge this fluid with positive and negative energy, from the right and left nostrils as you breathe through Ida and Pingala simultaneously. That charged fluid then rises up the spine to activate the energy centers (chakras). When it reaches the brain it awakens dormant brain cells. As neurons are activated for the first time, you experience waves of expansion. It feels like a hood surrounding your head. When energy rushes into Sushumna you are swept into total rapture, Samarasa. At that point, using an advanced technique, consciousness can leave through the Door of Brahma and soar into cosmic space.

Achieving Balance. Einstein received his Theory of Relativity intuitively (female), and had the mathematical skill to express it intellectually (male). That is true genius. Breathing simultaneously through Ida and Pingala equalizes the use of the right and left hemispheres of the brain. This is called the double breath. You learn to balance the energies by practicing Nadi Soghana, the Breath of Union, one of the most important techniques on the path toward Cosmic Consciousness.

When illumination occurs (See Tantric Marriage, Lesson 5) those two hemispheres, which had been operating independently of each other, undergo a neural transformation. A set of nerves comes into play which connects them, and allows them to communicate with each other, to work cooperatively instead of alternately.

Every physical disease and mental disorder involves an imbalance in male and female energies. Restoring that balance has tremendous healing value.

The flow of breath follows a succession of cycles described in the tantric system of Swara Yoga. It is a science of consciously patterned alternate nostril breathing. Normally a person breathes about 15 times per minute, or 21,000 breaths each day. There is a natural alternation back and forth between the nostrils, each being dominant for about 45 minutes. As dominance is switching from one to another, there is a moment of balance.

During the day more prana flows into the energy pathways of the brain. The concentrated flow descends along the right side of the spine and is solar. From midday, the prana flows up the left side of the spine and is lunar. This happens because the first six periods are controlled by the sun and the next six periods by the moon. For this reason midday and midnight are the two times of greatest balance between solar and lunar pranic energy currents, which produces a stronger Kundalini flow in the Sushumna. These are the best times for the Cosmic Cobra Breath Meditation.

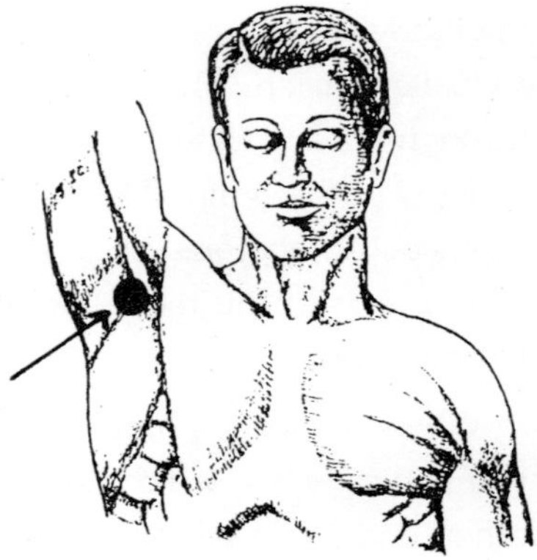

You can control what energy is manifested by choosing which channel to use. If you wish to be more intuitive (female), block the right nostril with your finger or a wad of cotton and breathe only through the left. If you need to be more analytical (male), then breathe through the right nostril only. You can turn your head to the right to stimulate the left nostril and vice-versa.

You can also suppress the active nostril by pressing your thumb directly on the main nerve in the armpit on the active side. Yogis carry a little stick for this purpose.

Another technique for opening both nostrils simultaneously is to do a scissor kick. While lying face down, swing your feet out until you feel a little pull, then swing them back to cross each other. Repeat for 5-10 minutes. Not only will the nostrils balance out, but you will also find congested sinuses open up.

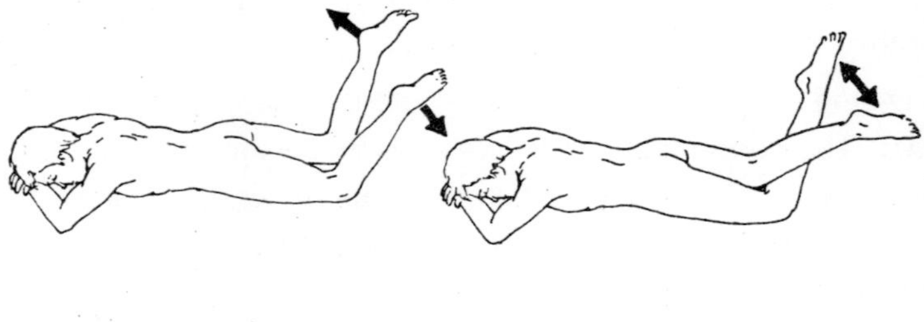

By controlling the flow of breath we control the manifestation of Kundalini Shakti (life-force) in our body. The deep breathing of the Complete Breath, the Breath of Union, and the Charging Breath, performed before the Cobra Breath, supercharge the respiratory, nervous, venous and meridian systems with life-force. This increases each cell's ability to infuse more prana and excrete waste products, which in turn brings prolonged and more energized life.

The techniques of tantric Pranayama join the mental faculty of awareness with flows of life-force in our bodies. When we become aware of the breath, it changes by itself. It slows down and becomes longer and deeper and floods our subtle energy circuits (nadis) with the fiery essence of Kundalini shakti. By learning to become more aware of the breath, we become more aware of life.

The Vishnu Yantra, or Star of David, depicts the union of male and female, of mind and body. This is the yantra we use to stimulate the heart chakra, the balancing point between the three lower (physical) chakras and the three upper (spiritual) chakras.

The Tantric interpretation of that symbol sees the six points of the star as the primary sexual organs.

The word "sex" comes from the Latin "sexus", which means division. The material world exists because of the interplay of electrical (male) and magnetic (female) energies, the oscillation between expansive centrifugal forces (male) and contractive centripetal forces (female).

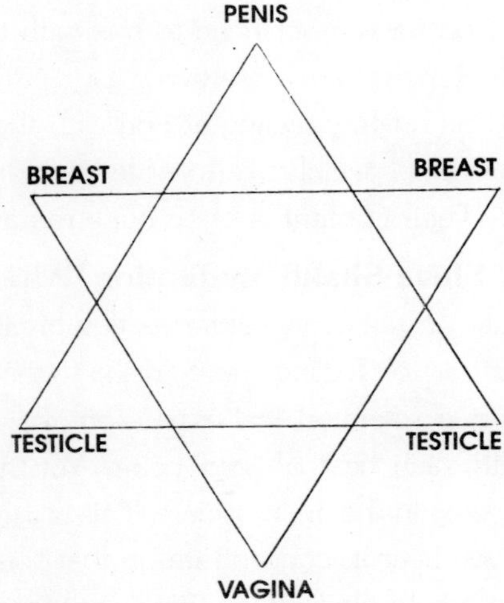

When the polarity between male and female merges in sexual union, we glimpse for a moment the return to the Eternal One.

Individual Practice

1. Balancing the Third Eye. The third eye is the masculine portal to Ajna, the 6th chakra. The medulla oblongata is the feminine entrance. By bringing their opposite and complementary energies together, you can experience the true color of Cosmic Consciousness.

1) Imagine a shimmering golden ball of light in front of your forehead. As you inhale through the nose, feel that energy being drawn in through the Third Eye to the center of your head, bringing its warmth and radiance to the Cave of Brahma. Exhale gently, leaving that golden light in your brain.
2) Repeat four more times, each time increasing the intensity of the golden light.
3) Imagine a ball of silver light at the back of your neck. As you inhale, feel that energy being drawn in through the medulla oblongata (the point where the skull rests on the spine) to the center of your head to mix with the golden light.
4) Repeat four more times.
5) Sit quietly, feeling at one with the Cosmos.
6) Take special care to note your dreams after doing this process. Their content is often quite remarkable.

2. Shiva-Shakti Meditation. While doing this meditation, concentrate on the brow center as you breathe. With each inhalation, concentrate on feeling energy rising to that clairvoyant center of the mind. During retention feel expansion like a sun radiating in all directions with each beat of your heart. You might hear or feel a ringing or buzzing in the brain or ears. This is the Nada (Cosmic Sound Current). If you hear it, concentrate on that sound while continuing to practice the breath meditation. The experience will join Consciousness (Shiva) with Energy (Shakti) and expand both as they become one in enlightenment or union with the Cosmic Breath of Life.

Part A. OM Yogic Breath

1) Start slowly by inhaling into the abdomen, then the chest, then the throat and head.
2) When pressure is felt in the lungs, exhale first from the head, then throat, chest and abdomen, releasing the smallest possible amount of air necessary to chant OM through the nostrils. This OM vibration in the nostrils causes an intense vibration in the sinuses and the fourth ventricle of the brain.
3) Repeat for five minutes.

Part B. Nadi Soghana - Breath of Union

Nadi Soghana is the principle technique for balancing male and female energies. It is also a simple natural method to take energy out of the head and diffuse it through the body. It is very effective in curing a headache and calming the nerves.

1) Focus on the Third Eye. Use Gyana Mudra in the left hand (hand on the knee, thumb and index finger connected). With the right hand, place the index finger extended on the "third eye" (between the eyebrows), thumb and middle fingers on nostrils.
2) Check to see which nostril you re breathing out of predominately. The main purpose of Nadi Soghana is to bring you into a balanced state of awareness so you start breathing equally through both nostrils. Press the dominant nostril closed with the thumb and exhale forcefully through the other nostril. Inhale through that nostril to the count of seven.
3) Close both nostrils and hold the breath for the count of seven. (Some people feel a twinge of panic when their nostrils are closed off. That panic will interfere with the practice. So, if you prefer, simply rest the fingers on the nostrils as a reminder not to breathe).
4) Release the right nostril and exhale through the right nostril for the count of seven.
5) Keep the left nostril closed and without pause, inhale slowly

through the right nostril to the count of seven. Contract the anus.

6) Close both nostrils and hold for the count of seven. (Or just use fingers as a reminder not to breathe.)
7) Release the left nostril and exhale through the left nostril to the count of seven, relaxing the anus.
8) Repeat the sequence seven times.

CAUTION: If you have high blood pressure, don't hold the breath.

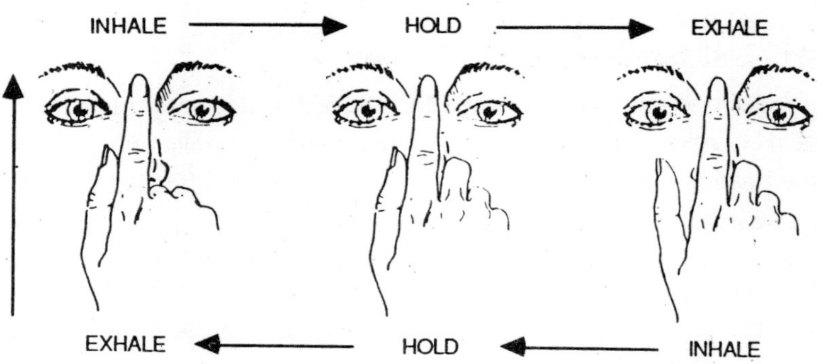

Part C. Yoni Mudra Meditation

Yoni Mudra means "Cosmic Womb" or "The Source of Existence." It is a powerful technique for sense withdrawal, allowing the mind to turn inward and observe itself. This should be done for five to fifteen minutes a day. You will notice after practice a feeling of tranquility, and that colors appear brighter.

1) Raise the elbows level with the shoulders and at right angles with the body.
2) Close the ears by inserting thumbs.
3) Close the eyes with the forefingers, placing fingers along lower lids
4) Place the middle fingers on either nostril to close the nose while retaining the breath (or as a reminder not to breathe).

5) Press the upper lip with the ring fingers. Press the lower lip with the little fingers.
6) Inhale slowly and deeply. Close the nostrils and retain the breath for as long as is comfortable, concentrating upon any visual images, spots or colors that may arise. You might begin to hear your internal sounds, which some refer to as "divine music." Release the nostrils and exhale.

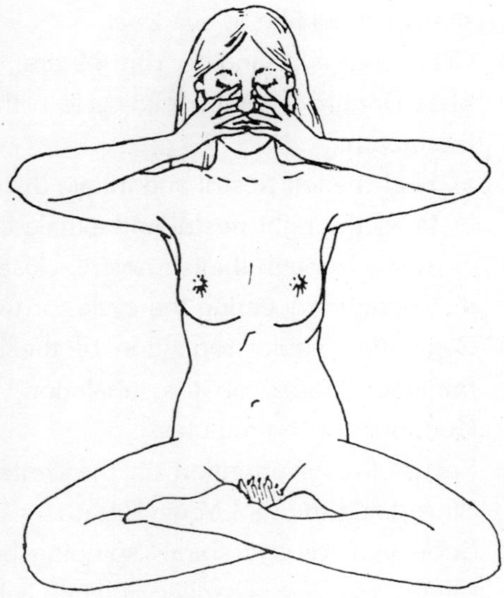

3. Advanced Shiva-Shakti Meditation. Return to this advanced form after mastering the Hong-Sau meditation, Lesson 8.

We use the crown chakra mandala symbol to unite the negative/positive (Shiva-Shakti) energy flows. We tune in to the essence behind the Chitti (mindstuff) which generates these flows and we balance them by turning the mind back on itself, stilling it and ultimately, transcending it.

This Shiva-Shakti mandala represents and activates the crown chakra, and will bring about psycho-luminescence in your head, like the sun radiating in all directions.

1) Sit in a comfortable position about 3 feet from the mandala. The symbol should be at eye level.
2) Close your eyes and do Yoni Mudra.
3) Start Breath of Union mid-cycle with no counting, no holding the breath.
    a) Shut the left nostril and inhale through the right.
    b) Press the right nostril and exhale through the left.
    c) Inhale through the left nostril, close it, open right and exhale.
    d) Continue repeating the cycle for two minutes.
4) Begin the mental repetition of the breath mantra Hong-Sau, thinking "Hong" on the inhalation, "Sau" on the exhalation. Continue for ten minutes.
5) Focus all your attention on the center of the mandala (Bindu). Start doing the OM Yogic Breath.
6) Soon you will see spirals spinning both left (Shakti) and right (Shiva) and silver sparkles of white light circling around the center of the symbol.
7) Visualize the symbol turning into a tunnel, coming out around you until you feel you are inside it, moving toward that center of white light (3 - 5 minutes).
8) Start doing the basic Breath of Union with your eyes focused on the mandala. During the retention of the breath, close your eyes and concentrate on the after image of the symbol in your mind's eye. (7 times)
9) The mandala will turn into a tunnel of light and you may feel energy streaming in through the crown chakra, at the top of the head.

Couple Practice

1. The Polarity of Lovers shifts at the moment of orgasm. The man enters his female energy, the woman enters her male energy. He feels more passive and receptive, she feels more active and aggressive. Make love as you usually do and notice how you feel just after orgasm when the energy has shifted.

Many people reach for a cigarette right after orgasm. Not too surprisingly, that flips your energy back to normal. Some people want to go to sleep immediately. Is that to escape this unfamiliar energy? Men particularly are uncomfortable and feel vulnerable in their female energy. If that is true for you, be aware of it and decide if you are willing to acknowledge that discomfort, willing to stay with it just a little longer each time, until you are comfortable.

If you are a woman who usually feels abandoned when your lover falls asleep right at the moment you feel most like communicating, get in touch with how long you have put up with this and how much resentment you have been holding. Now is the time to talk about it. If your partner is unwilling to stay in that energy, there's no point in continuing a course in Tantra. You might consider finding a different spiritual path, or finding a new partner!

In Tantra the woman takes an active sexual role. If you, as a woman, are accustomed to waiting for your partner to initiate sex and allowing him to control the sexual activity, this would be the time to open up new possibilities.

Be the initiator. Try sexual positions where are you on top. Sometimes you have to control the movements to get the right stimulation on the Sacred Spot. If it feels strange, or if he feels threatened, notice that and communicate about it. Get used to sharing equally the active and passive roles.

Some people are more comfortable giving than receiving, some just the opposite. Don't let your relationship get stuck in one-way giving and taking. Eventually that creates resentment on both sides. Let each take a turn to totally give, and then totally receive. You might find you can give and receive at the same time.

2. The Ultimate Orgasm. This is an advanced technique you can come back to after mastering Lesson 9 and 10. Bring Yoni Mudra into your lovemaking. Let one partner lie on a bed with head hanging back over the edge. This causes a rush of blood (prana) to the brain which intensifies the experience. Do Yoni Mudra while your mate stimulates you, manually or orally. As climax approaches, take the Transmutation Breath and pull the orgasmic energy into your brain.

Awareness

1. Be Aware Which Nostril Is Dominant on a moment-to-moment basis. Test yourself by closing the right nostril and sniffing through the left, then closing the left and sniffing through the right. When you notice yourself behaving in a particularly aggressive way, check to see if your right nostril is dominating. If you are feeling unusually emotional, notice that the left nostril is open. Validate through your own repeated observation the truth of these principles.

2. Review All Your Major Relationships at length in your journal (beginning with your opposite sex parent). Notice who was the active force, who the passive. Did you change roles from one relationship to the next, or have you consistently been the dominant or receptive partner? Remember how your parents had it worked out. Does your pattern reflect theirs? If you are in a long term relationship has there been any shift in the polarity over the years, moving toward a neutral middle?

3. Make an Honest Assessment of your willingness to explore the other end of the continuum, particularly if you find yourself sitting on one extreme in a highly polarized position. Remember, the goal of Tantra is to transcend male/female duality, to become androgynous. Are you ready for that?

Lesson 5

Kundalini and the Cobra Breath

Kundalini has been variously called "creative sex energy," "coil power," "Shakti" and "serpent fire." The traditional yogic teaching portrays Kundalini as a serpent lying dormant at the base of the spine, at the junction of Ida, Pingala, and Sushumna, coiled 3 and 1/2 times. It can be awakened by Yogic practices. Once aroused, Kundalini begins to climb up the spine. As it passes through the six spinal centers (chakras) it brings them to life, along with the psychic powers (Siddhis) which each chakra governs. They say that when Kundalini Shakti reaches the crown of your head she joins with Shiva in joyous reunion. You have attained liberation and are capable of performing miracles.

Awakening Kundalini Is the Primary Purpose of Human Incarnation. Many methods of stimulation have been used. One popular guru has his students bouncing on their buttocks and hyperventilating. A tremendous force builds up and the energy starts shooting up the spine in an uncontrolled way, sending dangerous shock waves through the body.

Another prominent guru has thousands of American devotees who will testify that he awakened Kundalini in them by his Shaktipat initiation, with nothing else required on their part except surrender to the guru's grace. This has become the latest rage and now many teachers are advertising that they give Shaktipat. It's a simple psychic trick and the results are very short-lived.

The Hindus tie a tuft of hair, an initiation knot, at that spot on the skull called Bindu; the place which is soft in babies and the very old; that spot where the soul is said to enter and leave the body. The initiation knot helps them to focus their consciousness on that spot. Then they feel the Kundalini spiraling energy all the time.

In tantric practice we learn that arousing yourself sexually and then using the breath as a vehicle, you automatically begin to feel the Kundalini force. Each tantric technique produces a certain repeatable experience, because Tantra is an exact science. Every time you do the technique you will get a similar effect.

Is Kundalini Dangerous? Critics of these practices have characterized Kundalini yoga as diabolical mysticism which produces physical pain, depression, and madness. Even Yoga teachers have represented Kundalini as a fiery energy that rushes up the spine, causing hallucinations and insanity. That is just a device to keep people who aren't sincere from playing with the energy.

There is nothing alien about this force. Kundalini is creative energy, the energy of self expression. It is simply your potential consciousness. Without it you could not function in the world. Most of us operate at a very low level of consciousness, so a sudden rush of expanded consciousness can be unsettling, especially if there is a lot of repressed material you are not willing to be conscious of.

It is true that if you aren t prepared for this experience, you could hurt yourself. It is essential that you clear your primal emotional issues, bring the repressed, sub-conscious feelings into consciousness, before Kundalini is activated.

You are given techniques to purify the physical body and the etheric body to prepare you to receive this rush of energy. The processes to delve into subconscious repressed material are given to prepare your mind for sudden flashes of insight. This preparation is important. One is well advised not to take short cuts. We have tools to accomplish that quite rapidly. This is the task of the Second Level Cobra Breath.

The "fiery furnace" is a code name for the emotional purification process that has been known for thousands of years. We are fortunate to live in a time when our technology allows us to translate the esoteric tradition into psychological and physiological phenomena. The entire Kundalini experience can be explained in neurophysiological terms (though that is beyond the scope of this book) as further demonstration that everything is contained within you. There is nothing outside of you. Simply allow what is already there to unfold.

Prana Shakti at the Base of the Spine is the key to our development. We learn to stimulate the shakti, magnetic energy and pull it in to charge the cerebro-spinal fluid in the sacral reservoir. We then draw that energy up the spine. Stimulating the base center activates centers in the brain, but it's easier to feel the sensations at the base, where the energy is more dense. Prana Shakti is not to be confused with Kundalini. Prana Shakti is magnetic. It feels diffuse like general light in a room. Kundalini is balanced energy and feels like a laser beam of coherent light.

We will learn Aswini and Vajroli Mudra, tensing the anal and genital muscles. This generates life force energy by stimulating the sexual glands. The energy locks (Bandhas) create a hydraulic pressure from the base center which pushes the energy up the spinal column, circulates it through the body and back to the genital area.

Shiva Kundalini Resides in the Brain. The ventricles of the brain are reservoirs for the cerebro-spinal fluid, just as is the sacral reservoir. Most Yogic schools only teach about the Shakti Kundalini. Working to "awaken the sleeping serpent" in the base of the spine is a very slow, safe, process. Starting at the brain with the more subtle solar energy greatly accelerates the process, but can create problems for one who has not purified the lower chakras.

The Kundalini Circuit. You will experience the energy movement as a cool, lunar, magnetic energy going up the spine. It changes polarity when it gets into the head, and becomes energized to a bubbly, warm, solar, electrical energy going down. You will learn to balance these two currents — lunar and solar, cold and hot, female and male. In the Dakshina path of Kriya Yoga we call this self-intercourse, making love to yourself with your own psychic energy. In Tantra, we circulate this energy with a mate, progressing at an accelerated pace.

Using the Cobra Breath while making love twice a day gets this energy circuit flowing through the body in one week. Once you have the feeling of how the energy moves, drop the technique and just flow with the energy.

The Tantric Marriage. In the center of your head is the Cave of Brahma, a chamber filled with spinal fluid (anatomically, the third ventricle). It connects to two other chambers (the lateral ventricles), one in each hemisphere of the brain (male and female hemispheres). The floor of this chamber is the hypothalamus, the body's pleasure center, which regulates the autonomic nervous system, the body's female aspect. At the front of the chamber is the pituitary gland, master gland of the body. This will become the abode of Shakti. At the rear of the chamber is the pineal gland, where Shiva sleeps.

In the first seven years of life, the pineal gland functions as a control on the pituitary, but then it becomes inactive and loses most of its function. The pituitary emerges and our worldly personality develops. Pineal was the guru and pituitary was the disciple. When those roles were reversed, all mental and physical problems began. The Tantric Marriage reawakens the pineal, restoring its active role, so the body/mind returns to balance.

Kundalini only begins to rise in Sushumna when there is an exact balance between the solar energy in Pingala and the lunar energy in Ida. Pulled in the vacuum created by the Cobra Breath, the charged spinal fluid rises through the central spinal canal into the third ventricle, the Cave of Brahma. You can feel a thin line of energy from the coccyx to the medulla and straight across to activate the third eye. The Cobra Breath sets up a vibration which stimulates the pituitary and hypothalamus. You can feel pressure and feel vibration as a tingle in your head. Now clairvoyance sets in spontaneously and you can be a visual witness to the fireworks at the marriage celebration.

When this Shakti force hits the medulla oblongata, it stimulates the pituitary. After a few minutes you feel pressure at the medulla, and then a rush as the hypothalamus shoots a spark across the cave to awaken the pineal. You can see a pin-point of light in your mind's eye. This indicates that the pineal has been awakened. (Most meditators have seen the white light and they think that's the ultimate, but that's just the begining!)

With the stimulation from the hypothalamus, the pineal (Shiva) becomes aroused and erect. An electromagnetic arc develops between the two poles, (Shiva and Shakti), illuminating the cave. You will see flashing colors, violets and blues. The lights may flash from one side of the brain to the other as the lateral ventricles are illuminated, uniting the two brain hemispheres. The pineal (Shiva) gives off a hormone, a spiritual semen, a cosmic male seed,which the pituitary (Shakti) opens to receive. The Cosmic Womb is now impregnated

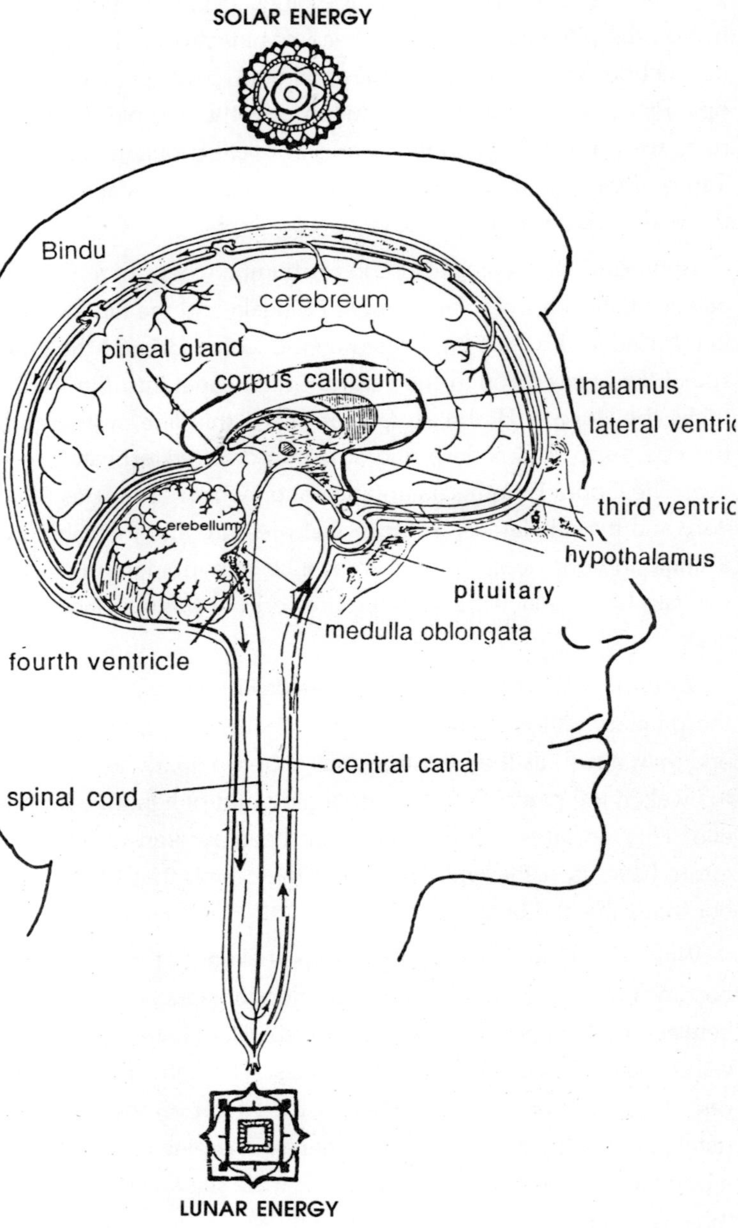
SOLAR ENERGY
Bindu
cerebreum
pineal gland
corpus callosum
thalamus
lateral ventric
third ventric
Cerebellum
hypothalamus
pituitary
medulla oblongata
fourth ventricle
central canal
spinal cord
LUNAR ENERGY

with the embryo that will develop into the Higher Self. This is the divine wedding where Consciousness comes into union with Energy to produce Cosmic Consciousness, a momentary glimpse of the Infinite. Visions may appear to you of saints, spirits, and gurus.

From this union emerges the androgynous Self, the realized spiritual being who knows its unity with God, your own personal guru, reborn by the Kundalini fire. With proper nourishment, regular meditation and conscious living, this embryo can grow and develop. Layers of ego will fall away like the serpent shedding his outgrown skin. When the transformation is complete, you will be a fully realized being, a radiant master.

The Key to Tantric Kriya Yoga is the Cosmic Cobra Breath, a very secret and sacred tradition, an oral teaching which cannot be written or recorded. It must be transmitted in person by those in the direct lineage from Babaji. Sunyata was authorized by his teacher to share this technique, and has authorized Bodhi and a few other carefully selected individuals.

This transforming process has been practiced in every advanced culture. Any system of self-development, if it is a true system, will have as its foundation a breathing technique similar to the Cobra Breath. The Cobra Breath is unique because it quickly produces the experience of Samadhi. It is not necessary to practice for years or undergo austerities or subject yourself to a guru. The key is learning to expand the breath.

"Pranayama" has been mistranslated as "control of the life force." In Tantra we don't control anything. We simply attune ourselves to the energies already present and encourage them to move more intensely. We are simply speeding up the evolutionary process. Pranayama is really "conscious expansion of the breath."

In many cultures, the snake, often a cobra, is used as a symbol of the Kundalini force, symbolic of expanding consciousness. Mind expansion feels like the hood of the cobra as it expands around you.

Our symbol in the Saraswati Order is a 3-headed cobra which represents the Ida, Pingala and Sushumna canals. When you do the Cobra Breath you feel the serpent energy, the cobra hood, opening up. Consciousness expands as the dormant brain cells start to open. You actually experience your etheric body and manifestations begin.

INITIATION

Initiation is a process whereby someone enters a particular spiritual path or system of self-mastery. Each path has its own unique vibration frequency. To follow a practice you must attune yourself to that frequency.

An initiator is one who has already tuned his body and mind to that frequency by following that path and experiencing its unique results. He is in a position to assist someone new in connecting with that energy.

Here are questions that are often presented, and some answers:

Kriya initiations are available through several schools and masters. Are they all the same? There is considerable variation between the Kriya teachings now available. The entire Kriya science was transmitted from Babaji to Lahiri Mahasaya, who transmitted it, in its entirety, to Sri Yukteswar. Students of Yukteswar received various aspects of Kriya, depending on their nature. Some were taught a devotional (heart) path, some an intellectual (mental) approach. This is the Tantric aspect of Kriya Yoga, the only one which utilizes the sexual energy. Even masters within the same branch teach different methods. There are hundreds of Kriyas. Each has a little different effect.

Is there more than one initiation? There are seven levels of initiation in this system - four of which can be given by an Initiator. The last three are received in meditation when you are ready for them. Each initiation is a variation of the Cobra Breath. Each takes you to a higher octave of the same frequency.

The first level Cobra Breath magnetizes the spine, opening the Shakti channel in the spine for earth energy to rise to awaken the 6th chakra. The second level opens the Shiva channel in the spine, allowing solar energy to descend, opening the lower three chakras, balancing the male and female currents. Third level opens the Sushumna Channel and actually allows the Cosmic Fire, a blend of the male and female, to ascend. The heart and throat chakras are opened and the entire chakra system brought into a balanced whole. The fourth level opens you from the microcosmic to macrocosmic, to the depths of earth and eternities of heaven. Higher levels must be experienced, and cannot be described.

Can I do the Cobra Breath Technique without initiation? Yes, and you would eventually get to the same place in your mastery. The advantage of an initiation is that it provides you with an immediate experience. Many people have a profound experience in initiation, which lets them know what is possible for them. It serves as a reference point later on as they work to rekindle that feeling. It's like a jumper cable that gives a jolt to your weak battery and gets you started. You can get there alone, but some of us don't have that much perseverance.

Does initiation involve me with a guru? The Kriya tradition had been lost to the world during the Dark Ages. It was restored by the Immortal MahaAvatar, Babaji. Born in 203 A.D., he was initiated at an early age into the mysteries of Kundalini Yoga. He retired to a Himalayan cave, absorbed in intense yoga practice, finally to emerge "laughing at the limitations of death." Babaji added his enhancements to the Kundalini Yoga, renaming it Kriya. He has retained his form through the centuries, guiding the spiritual development of those who seek his help. He is not at all interested in gathering a following, and lives in seclusion in the Himalayas, in an ashram known only to a few advanced students.

If you do the Cobra Breath, you automatically attune yourself to Babaji, as he is the physical manifestation of that energy. It is the purest expression of unconditional love. You might find, in deep meditation that you get a glimpse of him, or feel his presence. Some people need a guru-figure to assist in their spiritual evolution. You must find whatever is right for you

The Saraswati Order doesn't have just one guru. They respect all teachers. The goals of their path are personified by the Goddess Saraswati. She represents love, the arts, science and prosperity. Following these principles creates a balance.

Does initiation mean I belong to the Saraswati Order? No, that comes only after years of training at a Saraswati Ashram in India. Our initiation is available to those who have studied this course and decided to become part of this Ashram.

I'm already involved with another spiritual path. Will Kriya create a conflict for me? It might create a conflict for your teacher who wouldn't want to see you break with his tradition. Each guru line has its own vibration. There is a limit to how far each path can take you. For example, Mantra Yoga can only take you to the mental plane. Kriya Yoga is more powerful and takes you to a higher vibratory rate.

Many find that Kriya enhances their original path. It will certainly change you one way or another.

How does this initiation compare to Shaktipat? Kriya initiation stimulates the brain chakras. Shaktipat opens the emotional center—the heart. It can give you the experience of bliss and start your energy moving, but not your Kundalini. No one can stimulate your Kundalini except you (and your mate). Shaktipat, in most systems, binds you to a guru, holds you under his shadow. Tantra teaches you to be your own guru.

How do I go about receiving Tantric Kriya initiation?

1. Study this course and experience the practices.
2. Request an Initiation Application from the Ashram. See address on page 15. You will receive further instructions.

Individual Practice

1. Stimulating Kundalini. Two potent methods of stimulating Kundalini are:

1) Moving the sacrum (and pelvic bowl) forward and back, whether you are standing, seated or lying down, and
2) Contacting the anal sphincter muscle (for men) or the high vaginal muscles (for women).

Add these movements to any exercise or activity and you have made it tantric. Do them at the same time and you have turned on the energy generator.

2. Nadi Kriyas. The Nadi Kriyas are spiritual pranayama techniques (life-force expansion) to charge the physical body with prana. The Kriyas will remove any obstruction to the passage of energy and stimulate a high level of energy. This will strengthen the body, purify the blood and prepare you for Kundalini Meditation.

These three Nadi Kriyas should be done after the Rishi Isometrics postures and before meditation. Do each Kriya seven times. In each of these techniques, breathe in through the nose and blow out through pursed lips (as if about to whistle). With each inhalation, contract the anal sphincter muscle and rock the pelvis forward slightly. With each exhalation, relax the anal sphincter and rock the pelvis back slightly.

Part A. Nadi Cleanser: To unblock the nadi channels so energy can flow freely. This dispells fatigue.

1) Sit in the easy pose, or on a chair.
2) Inhale, rock forward, and contract for 6 counts.
3) Hold the breath for 3 counts.
4) Blow out with a powerful and steady force for 6 counts, rocking back and releasing the contraction.

<u>Part B. Nadi Activator:</u> Used after the Cleanser produces a rush of energy that stimulates the nervous system.

1) Standing with head and back straight, throw your shoulders back, rock the pelvis forward, tense your abdomen, anus/cervix, legs and knees.
2) Inhale a complete breath.
3) Holding the breath, extend both arms out in front of you shoulder high. Slowly clench your fists as you draw them back to your shoulders, tensing every muscle. Hold as long as possible.
4) Blow out explosively, drop the arms abruptly and relax the tension.

<u>Part C. Nadi Energizer:</u> Use when you feel sluggish. Vibrates all the systems (nadi, nervous, and vascular).

1) Sit in the easy pose.
2) Inhale in 6 vigorous sniffs, rocking the pelvis forward, contracting the anus/cervix.
3) Hold the breath as long as possible.
4) Blow out with a long slow sigh, relaxing contraction and rocking pelvis back.

3. Rejuvenation Postures, pages 113-120, done after the Nadi Kriyas, produces an energy rush that activates the Kundalini.

Couple Practice

Kundalini Massage

Massage can be as intimate an experience as a sexual encounter. The erotic aspect of massage induces a trance state of consciousness. Whenever you bring the erotic into any aspect of existence, you produce an altered state of consciousness. Out of the sensual arises the flow of the pranic forces up and down the spine. Massage is one of the easiest ways to get that energy flowing, particularly between a male and female, where there is polarity. Tantra Kundalini massage is a unique way of accomplishing this. There are many books available about sensual massage. They will not include these techniques.

Kundalini massage is a way for lovers to accelerate their spiritual evolution. The strokes serve to balance the male and female aspects (Ida and Pingala), which open up the Sushumna canal. At the same time, they stimulate the Kundalini to move up Sushumna from the base center to the medulla oblongata, the place in your body where the Breath of God comes in, the place where your OM starts. You will soon be able to send energy to your partner psychically, balancing the power centers to relax your mate before making love. A relaxed body can generate and transmute a higher intensity of sexual energy.

This massage stimulates the gonadal hormones, which stimulate the hypothalamus, which in turn releases hormones from the pituitary gland, the master gland. These hormones have a rejuvenating effect on the entire body and also aid in assimilating nutrients and eliminating toxins from the system.

The Western stereotype is that women like to be touched and men like to touch, reflecting our male active, female passive, polarity. Tantra doesn't bind people into such limited roles. Some men have to learn to enjoy being touched and some women must learn to be more active sexually.

A. Prepare to Give the Massage

1) Charge yourself with energy using Aswini Mudra to get your Prana Shakti flowing. (See Lesson 9)
2) Charge your hands by tensing them, talon-like as if holding a ball, and rotating them as you breathe deeply. On the exhale, project energy into your hands. Soon you can feel an energy field building up between your hands, something substantial that resists pressure.
3) The following is another very powerful way to pull the energy into your hands:

   a) Stand pigeon-toed, with sacrum tucked under. On inhale raise hands to the front to shoulder level, elbows close to body. Contract the anus.

   b) On exhale extend arms to sides. Make a soft fist with index finger pointed up. Feel a tingling in that finger.

   c) On inhale turn palms upward.

   d) On exhale relax arms to sides. Relax anal contraction.

   e) Repeat several times.

B. Giving the Massage

1) Place your sending hand (right for most people) on the coccyx and your receiving (left) hand at the top of your partner's head. Feel the vibrations in each center and the energy connection pulsing between them. Notice whether there is more energy in the head or tail, or if they are in balance.
2) Use a fairly strong percussion stroke on the triangular sacrum bone. Either tap with your fingers or the sides of your hands. See which feels best. The nerves that control all the organs in the urogenital system emerge from this portion of the spine. This stimulates the para-sympathetic system, (Shakti), inducing relaxation. It also serves as a wake-up call to Kundalini. The Kunda

gland, the body's connection to the infinite supply of Cosmic energy, is located just under the sacrum. Continue the percussion 3 or 4 minutes.

3) Generate heat on your partner's spine by creating dry friction. Using your giving hand, stroke repeatedly up the spine from the coccyx to the base of the skull with considerable pressure. Soon the spine, as well as your hand, will feel very hot. Focus between the shoulders to open the heart and throat centers. This arouses Shakti.
4) The trapezius is the muscle most in need of being relaxed. Much of your effort should be directed there. The tension comes from carrying too much responsibility on our shoulders. Also, working that area opens up the heart chakra, which is connected to and automatically opens, the base chakra. Squeeze and knead this muscle to coax it into relaxation. Massage the base of the skull (medula oblongata) with firm pressure.
5) Stroke up firmly on both sides of the spine, beginning at the coccyx with your thumbs crossed, right thumb on left side of spine, left thumb on right side. This serves to short circuit Ida and Pingala (i.e., neutralize the positive/negative energies). It is good for both of you to determine at this time which nostril is dominant and work toward equalizing the two nostrils, since only then does the Sushumna canal open up. As you stroke up the spine, both of you will take a Cobra Breath (once you have learned it). When you reach the medulla, do a small clockwise circular stroke and feather-touch back down as you exhale. Repeat several times.
6) To move the Kundalini, very slowly blow a stream of warm air up the length of the spine by placing one lip on one side of the spine, one lip on the other, both lips being dry. Breathe in through the nose and out through the mouth as you move your mouth from sacrum to base of the skull. You are creating a vacuum that draws the energy up. You will find one area, probably

the neck, that is especially responsive, creating thrills and shivers. Work there until the shivers stop.

7) Place the right palm over the sacrum, left hand at medulla, and hold for a few moments to balance the energy flow.
8) Invite your partner to roll over onto one side. Lie down behind, both facing the same direction, in the spoon position. Enfold your partner with your free arm, creating a protected nest.
9) Focus on each other's breath, synchronizing your breath patterns. Relax and enjoy the bliss of the eternal moment.

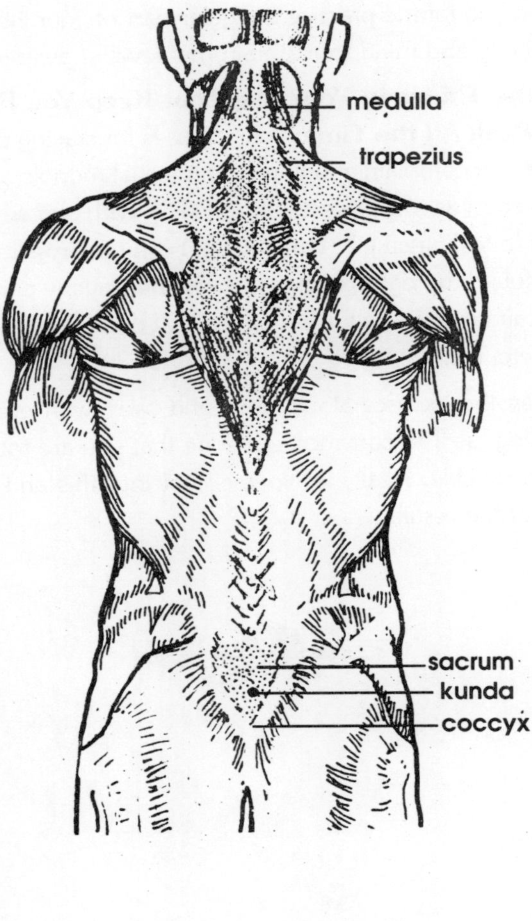

Awareness

1. Recall the Peak Experiences You Have Had: the moments when you felt most alive, most serene, most at one with the world, most in touch with God as you know Him. Realize that at these moments your body was going through the physiological process described above, that it had spontaneously achieved a balance of male and female energies and produced a Kundalini rush. Realize that you could have such experiences far more often by making meditation and tantric practice a regular part of your life, by preparing your body and mind to maintain that level of awareness.

2. List the Things in Your Life That Keep You From Being at Your Peak All the Time: your excuses for staying unconscious, the things you complain about in your internal monologue. "I will be serene as soon as this project is finished." "With a nose like this I'm supposed to feel blissful?" "I am loving. I can't express it yet because I haven't found the right partner." "After the way my parents treated me how can I ever hope for happiness?" "I don't deserve to be blissful." etc. etc. etc.

Now say the excuses aloud, over and over, with great and dramatic feeling, as if to convince someone that you are totally justified in being miserable. Really let yourself get into this and you will be surprised at the results.

Lesson 6

Awakening The Chakras

In the etheric body are energy centers called chakras. The chakras operate at a minimal level to sustain life in the spiritually undeveloped body. When Kundalini begins to move, the chakras come alive. It's like creating hydro-electricity when the pressure of running water rotates the dynamo.

The word chakra in Sanskrit means "wheel." The chakras are seen by clairvoyants as spinning whirlpools of energy, located along the spine (these are the negative or Material Chakras) and in the brain (the positive or Spiritual Chakras). Each chakra has a different rate of vibration, the fastest at the crown, and the others progressively slower, like transformers, stepping down the cosmic energy that enters the body at its crown. In the tantric chakra system, as devised by the yogis, the chakras are used as focal points in space to draw in the cosmic energy at the vital life-centers. With visualization you can actually open up the chakras, and with the movement of the breath, you can feel the energy traveling up and down the spine. When you work with the Kundalini circuits in the body, you stimulate each chakra.

Every Metaphysical Experience Can Be Explained in Physiological Terms. The chakras actually represent the endocrine glands which produce the hormones required to become conscious. Therefore when you learn to open up the chakras you become full of vitality, more alive, more intense, more focused.

The energy starts at the genitals and feeds to the other glands. When the endocrine glands are balanced and fully functioning, the aging process is reversed. In tantric practice you are in a constant state of rejuvenating yourself.

Initially We Bypass the Spinal Chakras. You have to be grounded to deal with the chakras because they contain all the unfinished emotional residue from your life. Opening them prematurely can cause unnecessary turmoil if you haven't yet learned to hold the Witness Consciousness as the emotional energy releases. Therefore in Kriya we open the brain chakras first.

The Cobra Breath is important because it brings to light all the psychic debris (which we call Samskaras). This is our karma, our habit patterns and conditioning we have picked up from our parents and society. By using the Breath and other tantric techniques, we can actually erase the grooves in the brain where such programming is stored.

First you must learn to energize the whole body so you can handle the input of energy coming through when the chakras start vibrating. Then chakras can safely be opened in a systematic way. Each spinal chakra has a spiritual counterpart in the brain. You first energize the brain, then you can safely transmute the energy back down the spine to start opening up the lower negative spinal chakras. The conscious breath draws from the Spiritual centers the power which manifests in the Material centers, supplying energy wherever it is needed. This opens up a journey into the various aspects of your personality, often a complete new world. Opening the chakras means seeing yourself as you really are, with no mask.

The Level Two work completes this process with the appropriate techniques and the support of a skilled counselor.

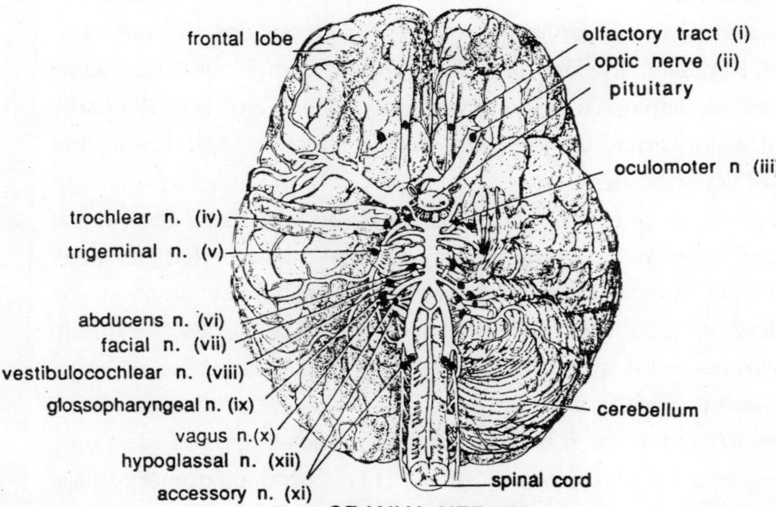

CRANIAL NERVES

There are 12 sets of cranial nerves that originate in a circle around the pineal. Each of these controls a body sense, including proprioceptive senses (awareness of position of the muscles). The psycho-luminescence in the third ventricle that happens when Shiva unites with Shakti alters these nerves and expands the range of the senses they control. Each chakra is associated with a sense, and in a body which has experienced Kundalini, each chakra has a psychic ability, an extrasensory ability.

There are many chakras in the body. In Tantra we recognize seven, each representing a different aspect of the human personality. A school of psychology has developed at each level of consciousness to explain human behavior as seen from that level.

Each chakra, then, is associated with an endocrine gland, with an element (earth, water, fire, air, ether), with a level of consciousness, with a sense, and with a dimension. (Many other associations have been drawn. These are sufficient for our purposes.) Let's look at the chakras one by one.

Muladhara. The first chakra is located in the prostate gland, for men, and near the cervix for women. Its stimulation activates the Shakti Kundalini, the life force, the energy by which our bodies were created. Muladhara rules the physical body. Its energy is of the earth and it is concerned with physical survival. Most people live at this level of consciousness, having no idea there is anything higher. They have no sense of adventure or willingness to take risks. Their main concern is to maintain the status quo, the behavior that has kept them alive thus far. Therefore their responses to any situation are predictable, robot-like. The Behaviorist Psychology describes their stimulus-response way of living. Sex at this level is instinctive, procreative, for survival of the species. This chakra is the transition from animal to human life. It is connected to the nose, and our basic animal urges arise, stimulated by smell. This is grounding energy. We can reach our spiritual branches up only as far as our roots are planted in the soil of Mother Earth. This is the bass viol of the human orchestra. We need its depth and richness to balance the flutes and violins of higher centers.

Swadhistana. The second chakra, associated with the testes or ovaries, is the home of unconscious emotional memories, both primal experiences from this life, and karmic residue from past lives. Its element is water. Here the awareness of self as an ego arises. The sense of taste is here and, as taste depends on smell, so the second chakra depends on the first. Life force expressed at this level sees the world in terms of pleasure and pain. Sex in this dimension is dedicated to sensual gratification. The Freudian view of human nature focuses on this level of consciousness. The sexual energy is the creative energy from which we sprang; the most powerful force we know; a great reservoir to tap. From this center one can experience clairsentience — reading the emotions of others.

Manipura. The third chakra is centered at the navel. This chakra is associated with vitality, energy and power. The main goal of life at this level is to be in control, to achieve, to win. Adler created a psychology on this premise. From this level, those who manipulate can "plug in" to people. They use their sexuality to control their partner, to barter for what they want. This chakra controls digestion and absorption of food and prana. It is associated with the pancreas and the adrenal glands which produce adrenalin to fire up the body. Fire is its element and it is the body's storehouse of cosmic energy. The nadis congregate here, creating radiant light. It rules the ego's Mental Body, the willfulness, the separate self.

Anahata. The fourth chakra is located near the heart. This center is associated with pure love and devotion. At this point ego boundaries start to melt away. There is a reaching out to embrace, to be at one with, the world. Carl Rogers' approach to psychology advocated unconditional love, which is only possible at this level of consciousness. The sense of touch is governed here and its element is air. This chakra is associated with the thymus, which controls the immune system, which produces cells that envelope and incorporate any foreign matter. Whatever seemed to be non-self becomes part of self. This chakra is usually heavily guarded. You have to go through a layer of pain, remembering all the times you needed love and it wasn't there for you. On the other side of that layer is the center where Atman, the Individual Soul, can be experienced.

Vishuddha. The fifth chakra, located at the throat, deals with dynamic communication and Self-expression. This is the center for purification, for preventing toxins from circulating through the body. Its gland is the thyroid. At this point the ego is able to step aside and let the cosmos express itself through that individual. Abram Maslow studied people who were able to achieve at super-human levels. To live in this consciousness is to know the Bliss Body. Its element is the ether, the essential stuff from which the other elements came. It is related to hearing and from this center you can experience clair-audience.

Ajna. The sixth chakra, the third eye, is associated with the pineal gland. Activation of the pineal and pituitary brings on the

"Tantric Marriage." This is the center of intuition and inspiration, beyond the material world, concerned only with the Cosmic Consciousness. Ajna is the connecting link between ego and the universe as it is directly connected to the lowest and highest chakras. When consciousness reaches this level, you connect with the Universal Mind and, seeing things as they really are, without an ego filter, you behold the divine in all of creation. Clairvoyance happens automatically, bringing clarity and insight into your perceptions about people. Once Ajna is open, no one can ever lie to you. You have tapped into the Collective Consciousness which Carl Jung studied.

Sahasrara. Each chakra is connected to Sahasrara. This is the center of Nirvanic Consciousness, our connection with the Infinite, the Void. This crown chakra is called the Thousand-Petaled Lotus. Its physical counterpart is the brain with millions of dormant neurons waiting to blossom. As you gain mastery over the Breath, more "knowingness" becomes available. As dormant potential begin to express itself, the brain feels like it's on fire.

Bindu. This is a secret chakra, the moon chakra. Located at the top and back of the head, where the hair twists, it is the place where the soul enters and leaves the body. Here you can tune into psychic sounds. Though it is not usually thought of as a chakra, it is probably the most important point in Tantra Yoga. The hypothalamus is associated with Bindu. It regulates the energy flow from the pineal to pituitary.

The first four chakras represent the aspects of our humanity, and must be mastered, and surrendered to the higher Nature, represented in the three higher chakras, spiritual centers which are past the material plane.

In the tradition, this esoteric information was portrayed in poetry and symbolism. Perhaps the Yogis in ancient times didn't have the vocabulary that we have now, and perhaps they wanted to keep the information guarded. They referred to the Chakras as lotuses, and

Nadis as solar and lunar currents. We have discovered that the neurons in the brain can be activated. That's where the Kriya breath comes in. We introduce more oxygen into our head. We are working with steps and degrees of awareness as a physical manifestation. When we talk about the chakras, remember we are talking about the brain. It all originates in the brain. All information is contained in the brain. Then it is transformed down by the chakras on the etheric level into the various emotional states.

SEQUENCE FOR OPENING CHAKRAS

1. Will or Witness? In most Yogic traditions, the first chakra to be opened is Manipura, the Vital center. This is because a strong will and self-discipline are required to follow the yogic life. This point is the reservoir where all vital energy is stored. Many tantric practices (asanas, pranayama, and mudras) are designed to strengthen the sexual glands to produce a tremendous force and psychic heat, to pull energy up from the base of the spine to open Manipura.

The Yogic Path of Will tends to ignore or suppress the emotional body. For those who follow the Path of Surrender and intend to master the emotional body, the Third Eye must be opened first. We can then learn to call in the Witness, our individual Soul, to maintain an objectivity while the emotional clearing takes place. The Witness is essential to that process. No amount of catharsis will release old emotional memories unless the Witness is present.

2. Emotional. We must then bring consciousness to the emotional memories in the lower three chakras, particularly in the Etheric (pranic) body, to release our attachment to them, to learn the lesson for which we created that experience. Western psychology has focused on this process and many methods are available. When approached in a spiritual context, these methods are enhanced. Then the goal is to integrate emotional fragments, to bring harmony between the body and mind so the body/mind can enjoy the Divine Presence.

3. Heart. If you open Anahata before the primal emotional material is cleared, you are setting yourself up for heartbreak. As long as you still have an emotional charge on the opposite-sex parent, any partner you choose would be someone who reminds you of that parent, an attempt to get from your partner what you didn't get from the parent, to complete that relationship. You don't see the partner, only your projection of the parent. Such an attachment is built on illusion, and usually falls apart. But if your heart is open, you would love that illusion unconditionally, and the breakup would be devastating. Once the heart is open, your capacity for real love and joy expands dramatically. Your Divine Essence can enter this physical temple and you become a Radiant Being.

4. Cosmic. The four lower chakras must be opened, the four dimensions they represent must be mastered, before you are ready to fully open the Cosmic Center. As your intuitive faculty opens up at Ajna, the third eye, you project your consciousness into the cosmic space, into the Godhead. The key that allows this journey to actualize is the Cobra Breath. It takes the energy up from a gross level to a more refined level which represents the God within us. The Breath comes up the spine and hits the medulla, which activates the positive brain centers. When the Cobra strikes the pineal gland, all the Spiritual centers start to vibrate and resonate and create an auric field around the body. We realize then that our sense of separateness was an illusion. There is only one Universal Soul that contains everything.

When we go through spiritual training and develop paranormal abilities, we tap into the Collective Consciousness. When we learn to be sensitive to more subtle energies, we can pick up on that particular frequency. The chakras transform that refined energy down into a frequency we can work with on the physical plane.

CHAKRA YANTRA MEDITATION

This marvelous exercise will give you three vital skills: 1) the ability to visualize; 2) a technique to simulate and balance your Chakras; and 3) the power to tap into the etheric energy body that surrounds you.

Visualization is essential to any esoteric study. It is the core of Sex Magick techniques you will learn at a more advanced level. To focus on a single point, like a candle or crystal, is a well-known way to gain control over the mind. But that is a passive practice which induces a form of hypnosis. Yantra Meditation is the basic tantric technique for learning to visualize. It is very dynamic. Tantra always looks for the most efficient ways to achieve its ends.

For those with artistic talent, visualization comes very easily. But those whose nervous systems are more oriented to sound or touch will take longer to master the skill. Don't be discouraged if it doesn't happen the first time you try. It's worth it to you to persist. A few years back, when people read for entertainment, they had to create their own mental pictures of the story. We who have grown up with a barrage of TV images may never have learned to make our own images. We can have a concept of something with a vague or hazy picture. These exercises will train you to create a visual image projected in vivid color and clarity on the screen of your closed eyelids.

You can obtain a set of yantra cards by sending in the coupon on the next page. The technique takes advantage of a physiological response to fatigue, called the After-image Effect. You focus your gaze at the Bindu dot in the center of the yantra for 1 to 3 minutes <u>without blinking</u>. You push yourself well beyond the normal limit for fatigue. The eyes will probably start to tear, but that is good because tearing produces a relaxed state in the body. When you reach a certain point of exhaustion the yantra will start looking 3 dimensional, and perhaps there will be flashes of colors. Then you close your eyes and in a moment you see the image floating in the darkness in front of you, in the color complementary to the one on the yantra. For example, gazing at a blue yantra would fatigue the blue receptors, leaving red and yellow to make an orange image. After some practice you learn to create this visualization without the help of the card.

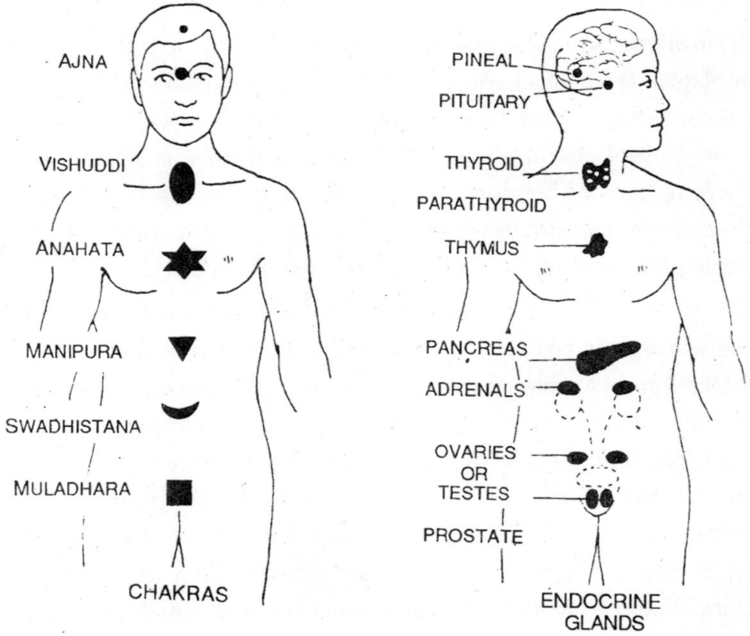

Stimulating the Chakras is accomplished safely and effectively using Yantra Meditation. Each Yantra is a geometric shape which represents a certain mantra, or word of power, which resonates through the nervous system. The Yogis discovered that for each chakra there is a particular mantra, a yantra and a color which are attuned to the chakra energy and therefore stimulate the chakra. When you have produced the image of the Yantra in your mind's eye, you can move it very gently, with the breath, to the location in the body to which it corresponds. Together with the mantra this produces a physical stimulation to the chakra. As you stare at Bindu, the dot in the center of the yantra, it also stimulates the Bindu chakra.

CHAKRA YANTRA SYMBOLS

Chakra	Location	Geometric Form	Color and Complement	Bija Mantra	Tantric Mantra	Element
1 Muladhara	Cervix or Perineum	Square	Orange(Blue)	Lam	Lang	Earth
2 Swadhistana	Base of Spine	Crescent	Silver(Black)	Vam	Wang	Water
3 Manipura	Navel	Triangle	Red(Green)	Ram	Rang	Fire
4 Anahata	Heart	Hexagon	Blue(Orange)	Yam	Yang	Air
5 Vishuddi	Throat	Oval	Violet(Green)	Ham	Hang	Ether
6 Ajna	Brow	SriYantra	Lt.Blue (Lt.Orange)	Om	Ang	Light

The Astral Energy, you will remember, forms an envelope around the physical body. Our spinal column is like an antenna that picks up energy at different frequencies in both the material and astral planes. While doing this meditation you contact the astral energy outside your physical body through the nervous system and learn to draw a particular frequency into your body. When you become sensitive to your subtle energies, you will know which chakra is stuck and needs a boost, or which is weak and needs energizing. Each vibration has a color which is a certain emotional state or level of consciousness and you can use the colors to discriminate which energy to work with. The color you draw in to you stimulates that particular emotional tone in your body. Chakras must be purified before Kundalini can flow. They are usually blocked or weak in energy.

The tantric masters devised yantras that were actually the complement of the astral colors. Using these reverse colors allows you to directly contact the astral energy, which is what connects the chakras to the central nervous system. This produces a more powerful stimulation of the chakras for faster development. Working with the astral colors in the tantric system is much more dynamic.

(The cards were devised by and for men. Women's color perception is different. If a woman sees colors other than specified on the chart, don't be concerned).

Each chakra also had a traditional bija mantra that yogis would chant to stimulate that chakra. Just repeating that transcendent sound over and over allows you to feel a vibration at the place in your body that resonates to the sound. Tantric masters developed a more intense version of that sound to accelerate the process. They changed the final consonant from an "m" to "ng" which brings the resonance higher into the head. This makes the head ring and connects each chakra to the 3rd eye.

For each mantra a certain pitch is most effective. Lower pitches work for lower chakras, higher pitches for higher chakras. Experiment with different pitches to find the one that is strongest for you.

By using the visual image and sound vibration together, you create a dynamic feeling inside your nervous system and open up another aspect of your being.

The technique of Yantra Meditation should be practiced for ten minutes each day, <u>one yantra per day.</u> After some practice you can dispense with the yantra cards and produce the image by internal visualization. You will be able to stimulate each chakra by mentally moving the yantra into its proper position along the spine. Focusing your attention on that area sends energy to it.

In Tantra this is called "Internalization of the Gods." The Yantras become like a living deity within the physical body. Each time you activate a chakra point, you bring into consciousness scenes of old repressed experiences, unforgiven grievances, primal fears, little hurts and insults, all come up to be bathed in the light of consciousness, to be experienced, Witnessed, and dissolved away.

This meditation is the safe and natural way to stimulate and harmonize the chakras. <u>Daily practice</u> will produce <u>immediate results</u>. Your progress will be very rapid.

Individual Practice

1. Charging Breath. (To bring quick energy into the brain)

Inhale through the nose with a sniff, throwing the head back. Exhale through the mouth, throwing the head forward, with a "ch" sound. Repeat rapidly 7 times. Take a deep breath, hold, and relax.

2. Mudras to Activate Chakras. When you have mastered these exercises, you can add the chanting and the yantra gazing.

1) Earth Center: Inhale through curled tongue (sita breath) while contracting the anus. Exhale doing slow, rhythmic anal contractions, (chanting ("LANG").
2) Sex Center: Inhale through nose, picturing the breath coming through the third eye. Gently visualize breath going down the frontal passage until it reaches the Fire Center. Then force air down and out the genitals. While exhaling, tighten anal muscle and visualize energy rising up the spine, (chanting "WANG").
3) Fire Center: Take a deep sita breath, filling up stomach area. On the exhale, forcibly contract the stomach (as you chant "RANG"). Try to pump 26 times during one exhalation.
4) Air Center: Breathe in through the nose. When breath reaches the heart area, contract and expand the chest muscles around the heart, (chanting "YANG").
5) Ether Center: Breathe in through the nose. When the breath reaches the throat center, do a chin lock. While holding the breath, raise the chin, still keeping the tension in the throat. Exhale, (chanting "HANG").
6) Light Center: Press index finger on third eye or index and middle fingers gently on each eyelid. Inhale through third eye. Feel energy move across psychic bridge to Bindu. On the exhale, (chanting "ANG"), project the energy back out through the third eye into the ethers.

3. Yantra Meditation.

1) Use the card for the first chakra on the first day, second chakra the second day, etc. Place the yantra at eye level. Have a candle or light on one side so that the yantra is illuminated.
2) Focus your gaze on the Bindu point in the center of the yantra. Don't allow yourself to blink. Intone the Tantric Bija Mantra for that center over and over again. Do this for 1 - 3 minutes. Focus your mind completely on the yantra and mantra.
3) Close your eyes and mentally visualize the yantra floating before you, silently repeating the mantra.
4) Internalize the yantra symbol. Gently inhale the image, first to Ajna center, then guide it with the breath to its appropriate location on your spine. Be aware of the stimulation for as long as possible.

Couple Practice

Kama Marmas are erogenous zones to stimulate the physical body and nourish the psychic body. They are all chakras and sub-chakras. In sex worship, these various Kama Marmas are kissed, caressed, anointed with oils and perfumes, adored with the eyes, etc., to turn the entire body into an erogenous zone.

A traditional pattern is to first touch, then blow, then lick each part in turn. That is not a rigid formula, but each step produces a unique response and you don't want to miss any of it.

To proceed most effectively, start at the Secondary Zone, then the Primary and finally the Tertiary. When all have been awakened you can go wherever you wish. The left side of a woman's body is usually the most sensitive, and the right side of a man's body.

TANTRIC EROGENOUS ZONES

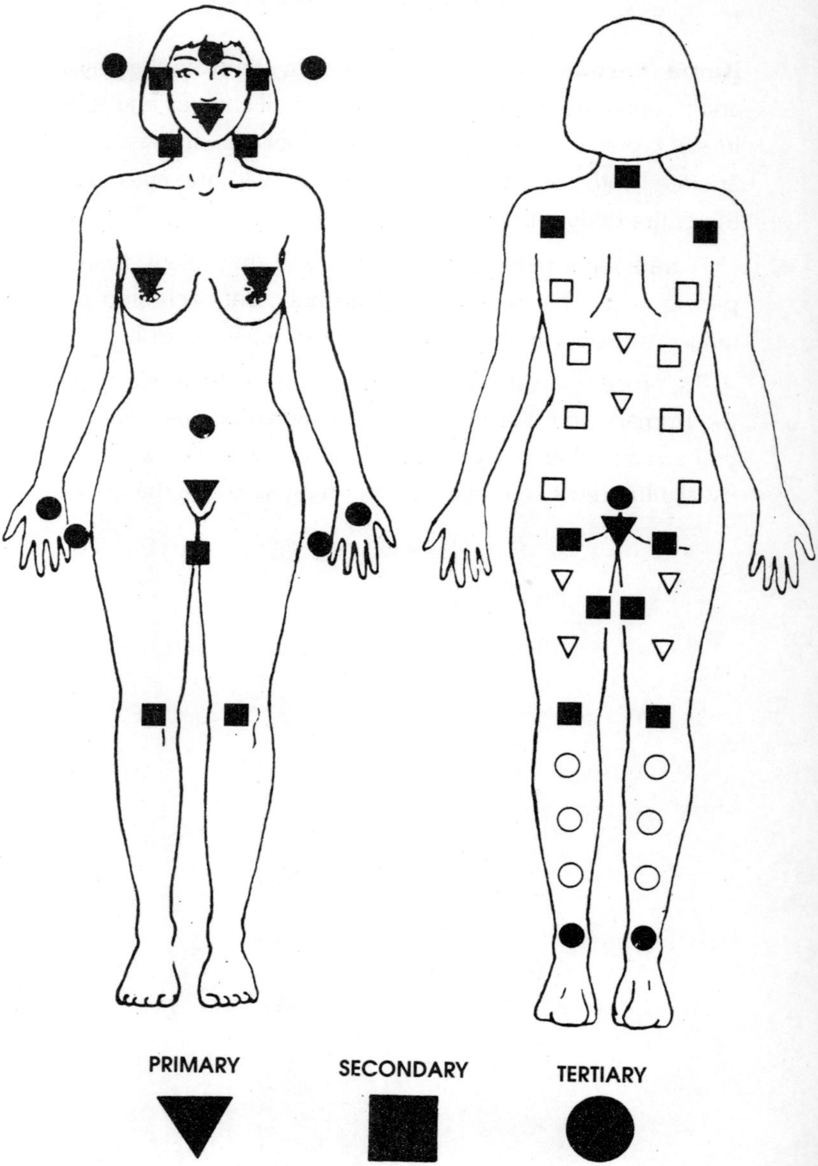

Erotic Massage (Charging the Chakras).

Primary Level

1) Lips (and the labia). Tongues must unite as well as lips.
2) Breasts, nipples. The nipples radiate psychic energy, and also "breathe energy in" to nourish the heart chakra. Nipple stimulation opens up the Third Eye and causes an erection.
3) Genitals. In a woman, her clitoris is the key to her autonomic nervous system; in a man, the tip of his penis.

Secondary Level

1) Earlobes. Stimulates 1st chakra. First left earlobe to open Ida, then right for Pingala. Tingles go directly to uterus.
2) Nape of the neck. Opens up throat chakra and Sushumna.
3) Sacral-Lumbar junction. Stroking opens up first two chakras and triggers reflex to genitals.
4) Gluteal fold (where leg meets hip). Opens up first chakra.
5) Inside of thighs. Very light stroking up to the genitals opens up 2nd chakra, and causes scrotum to draw up.
6) Back of knees. Stimulates knee chakras and is most delightful.

Tertiary Level. (These points are usually dormant until Secondary and Primary zones have been stimulated, although a new compatible partner might elicit an instant tingle here.)

1) Edge of little finger. Gentle strokes sends tingle to spine.
2) Palms of hand. Sensitive to circular stroke.
3) Navel. Gentle clockwise stroke opens up Manipura.
4) Anus. Direct connection to 1st chakra. Exquisite pleasure.
5) Nostril. Opens Ajna. Stroke, nibble, lick sends out thrills.
6) Ear orifice. A trance can be broken by blowing sharply into the ear.
7) Soles of the feet.
8) Big toe. Sucking can induce orgasm in some people.

Awareness

1. Become Aware of Your Chakra System. Be clear which level of consciousness dominates your life. Know where you are stopping the energy. Begin to ask why you won't allow that aspect of you to express itself.

2. Be Aware of Feelings that come up through the day. It's easier to Witness thoughts. It's harder to step back from emotions. But you'll get the knack. As feelings come up, don't push them back down. Take a deep breath. Feel the emotions totally, and watch yourself feeling them from a detached vantage point. It's just like watching the breath. You needn't do anything. It fixes itself. Old fears and hurts, experienced CONSCIOUSLY, WITHOUT JUDGEMENT, lose their power over you, begin to fall away.

3. Let Go of Your Psychic Debris. As painful memories come to mind, take yourself into the Bindu space with the people for whom you have emotional charge. Realize that they were specially selected by Existence because they were perfectly suited to be your teachers. If there are many of them, it is because you are a slow learner and Existence had to present you that experience over and over until you learned the lesson. Bless these people for being exactly the way they were. Forgive them for what their unconsciousness did to you. Forgive yourself for taking so long to see the lesson. Be grateful to Existence for its perseverance.

Lesson 7

Tantric Rejuvenation System

The human bio-energy system is a multilevel system. We work with the gross physical body (with chemical processes activating its network of cells and organs) and the etheric energy body or aura (with prana activating the Kundalini moving through the chakras). Other levels are spoken of by mystics, but bringing these two bodies into balance is sufficient to achieve transcendence.

This is an Ancient System of Rejuvenation which has kept many yogis in perfect health well past the 100 year mark. It is based on intense stimulation of the endocrine glands. As we have said, the endocrine glands are, to the physical body, what chakras are to the etheric body. All the techniques presented in this course to stimulate the chakras also stimulate the endocrine glands. Techniques include: breath, cleansing the nadis, moving energy, massage.

The endocrine glands are different from other glands in the body in that they are ductless, that is, the hormones they produce are released directly into the bloodstream and so affect the entire body. The glands are closely related. A weakness in one gland will draw energy from the others. They serve to stimulate and repress each other to maintain balance. When all the glands are producing hormones at their optimal rate and in perfect balance with each other, the body does not age.

Those hormones are also essential in preparing the body to receive the Kundalini experience. You must be in optimal health for awareness to manifest. Otherwise you can't handle the energy. In Tantra we start at the physical level, working through sexual union to stimulate the sexual hormones. A high level of energy in your sexual glands is prerequisite for the tantric experience. Their energy can be distributed throughout the body to prepare it for Universal Consciousness.

Each chakra produces a "vortex energy field," and, in a healthy normal person, spins at a great speed, controlling the psychic energy in the body. As we grow older, burdened by the stress of modern living, some chakras slow down so the energy goes out of balance. This leads to deterioration of the health of the body, and ultimately to its death.

This series of exercises is simple to do and requires only ten minutes to complete, once you become proficient. The exercises stimulate the circulation of oxygenated blood through the entire body and balance the life-energy in the chakras.

Some of these movements may look like something you have done in the gym, but this is not a program for muscle toning or aerobics, although that might happen as a side-effect. This program is expressly for balancing and stimulating the chakras (endocrine glands).

The postures are designed to return the energy body to a balanced state, restoring the rate of spin of the chakras to the level of a normal twenty-five year old person. If the balance of the energy body is maintained over a period of time, it will affect the physical body, causing the glands to once again secrete in perfect balance those hormones which are the key to radiant health and vitality.

The Kaya Kalpa System for rejuvenation is a much larger practice that is integral to the advanced practice of Kriya Yoga. "Kaya Kalpa" means "Body Immortal." The full Kaya Kalpa regimen is carried on during ninety days of seclusion. It must be under the guidance of an experienced Ayurvedic doctor, as it involves the use of potent herbs and narcotics. Alchemical formulations of mercury, and other substances which could be poison if prepared incorrectly, serve to restore an aging body to its prime. Also there are some exotic practices which we mention for completeness, but don't recommend outside the monastery setting. This includes such things as drinking urine and menstrual blood. The "Tantric Milkshake" consists of a mixture of semen and vaginal secretions, an extremely nourishing tonic. That same mixture can also be applied as a facial mask with remarkable rejuvenating effects on the skin.

These practices may seem extreme, but the stakes are high. Yogis who are advanced in the practice of Kaya Kalpa are searching for immortality of the physical body and some have attained it.

Needless to say this whole training is underground and very secret. The ego is fascinated at the thought of immortality and would go to any lengths to learn how to accomplish this. The methods are only made available to those who have transcended ego, who genuinely want more mortal time to finish their spiritual journey.

Dietary Considerations. There are many books available about improving your diet. That's a subject too big for this brief discussion. But here are several important things you can explore:

1) Mix honey and ghee (clarified butter) in equal amounts. Take 1 tablespoon each day to lubricate the internal organs and give a glow to your skin.
2) Solar foods are the basis of many rejuvenation systems as the energy of the sun has life-giving power. With modern technology we have discovered that the chlorophyll molecule is capable of capturing the sun's energy. The food highest in chlorophyll, the most potent rejuvenator you can ingest, is wheatgrass juice. We have observed grey hair returning to black in a period of several weeks, chronic aches and pains disappearing, improved energy and vitality that is startling, just from drinking 2-3 ounces of fresh wheatgrass juice each day. It speeds healing from any injuries or infections, reverses the course of degenerative diseases, detoxifies, and even protects you against radiation.
3) Get tested for food sensitivities, either in a laboratory or by

kinesiology, radionics, or pendulum. If you are constantly subjecting your body to foods it considers toxic, you put a great deal of unnecessary stress on the immune system.

4) Dehydration is one cause of most degenerative diseases. Drink two quarts of spring water daily. Salt regulates the body water levels, but normal table salt has been heated and its crystal structure distorted so it doesn't perform its function and most people are chronically dehydrated. Use only sea salt or kosher.

The Rejuvenation Postures are now being included in many books and systems. They are called the Tibetans or The Five Rites of Rejuvenation. The man who originally brought them to England from Tibet unfortunately left out the most important aspect of the system, the one detail that makes the movements really effective.

If you do an anal contraction with each exhalation, you stimulate the Prana Shakti energy. Releasing that contraction on the inhalation propels that energy into the body. Coordinate the breathing with the movement, one breath per repetition. Breathe in through the nose and out through the mouth to purify the body.

When you do the postures you will feel a charge of energy — a real Shakti rush. Sometimes it is too much and creates a feeling of nausea as the channels are being cleared. Pace yourself and do just as much as you can without going over your limit. Each movement is a meditation. Focus your attention on the movement and energy.

Individual Practice

1. Shiva-Shakti Mudra. We begin with the physical discipline of the postures to get energy flowing. Then we distribute the energy through the body by doing 3 repetitions of the following mudra. Breathe through the nose, slowly, conscious of the energy being moved.

1) Stand with feet shoulder width apart, knees slightly bent, back straight. Inhale as you lift your hands, palms up, to the front at waist level, elbows close to the body. Feel that you are drawing energy up from the earth.
2) Exhale as you push the hands out fully to the front, at shoulder height, palms forward and vertical. You are giving the energy back to the world.
3) Straighten the wrists and inhale as you raise your arms overhead, palms open to the heavens (arms at 10:00 and 2:00).
4) Exhale as the arms come down (very slowly and consciously) in two large arcs. Palms toward the body, the hands pass each other before your face and again at the genitals. When the hands cross, don't allow them to touch since that would short circuit the energy. Feel their energy as they pass the genitals.

2. Rejuvenation Postures. Each posture is eventually to be performed 21 times, and no more. In the beginning do as many repetitions as are comfortable, at a rate of speed that feels right for you. Some people can do them very rapidly, some like to go very slowly. If you can't do that many, or if you can't reach the full position, don't worry. With practice your muscles will become stronger and more limber and your energy will increase.

Assume the "Star Position" with feet wide apart and arms extended at shoulder height. Turn your left palm up and your right palm down. Feel the energy flow into your upturned hand, through your body and out through your downturned palm, back to the earth. If this doesn't feel right to you, reverse the palms. Some people receive through their right hand and send through their left hand. The energy coming from above will feel hot, the energy returning to the earth will feel cool.

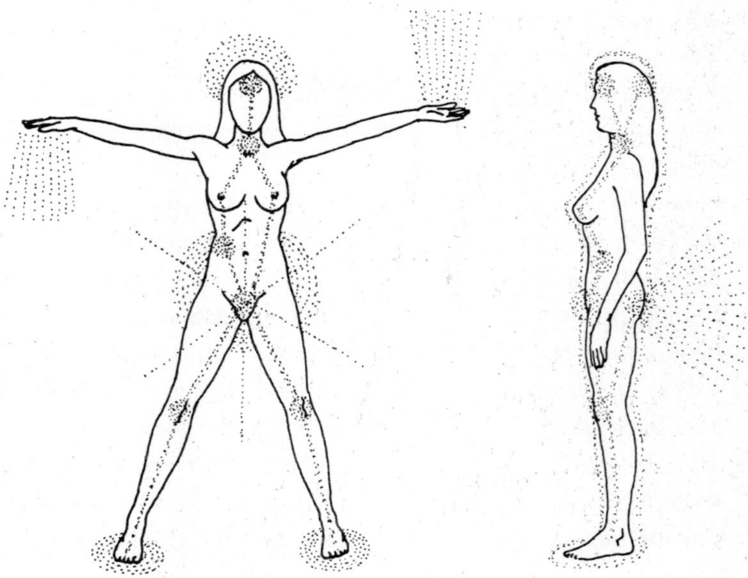

The vortices these exercises affect most are those related to the knees, the sex center (gonads), the liver/spleen, the throat (thyroid), and two in the brain (pituitary and pineal glands).

Part A. The first movement is spinning, similar to the whirling dervishes of Persia. It serves to speed up all the chakras, particularly those in the knees.

1) Extend the arms horizontally to the sides, with the receiving palm up and the giving palm down. (If space is limited, left hand can go straight up, right hand straight down, palms facing up and down, respectively.) Then spin at your own speed in a clockwise direction (with the right arm going backwards). Pick out an object in the room to focus on, and count every time the eyes return to that object. Spin until you become slightly dizzy, but no more than 21 times. Breathe normally.
2) To remove dizziness, arms still extended, make soft fists, pointing the index fingers up. With both index fingers in your peripheral vision, arc your arms toward the front at eye level. When they meet in front, pull the hands in toward the heart, as you look directly at them. The dizziness will disappear.

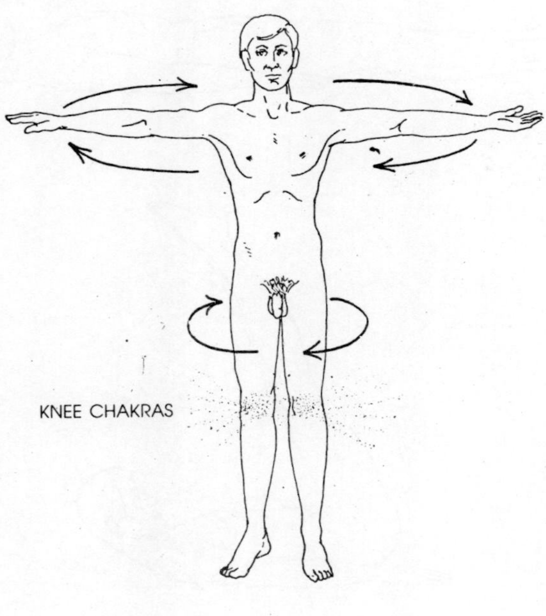

Part B. This exercise serves to stimulate the throat and sexual center.

1) Lie on your back, legs straight, hands under the buttocks, palms down. In one coordinated motion, as you exhale (mouth) and contract the anal sphincter/cervix, the legs and head are raised simultaneously. The knees are kept straight, legs together, as the feet are brought over the head. The chin should be pressed to the chest. Keep the hips on the floor.
2) As you inhale (nose), slowly lower the head and legs to the floor and for a moment allow all the muscles to relax.
3) Repeat as desired, up to 21 times.
4) Do 3 Shiva-Shakti Mudras.

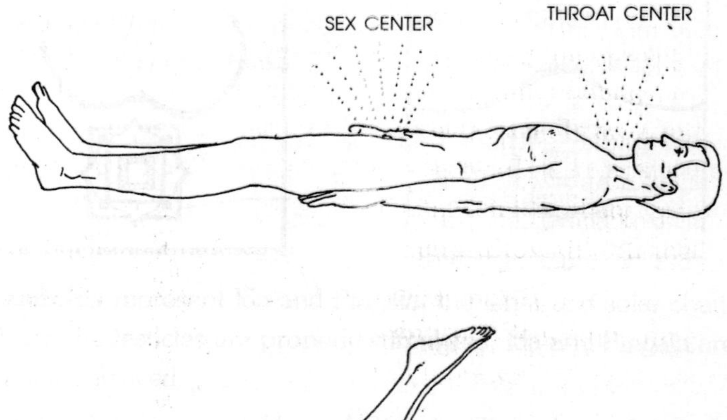

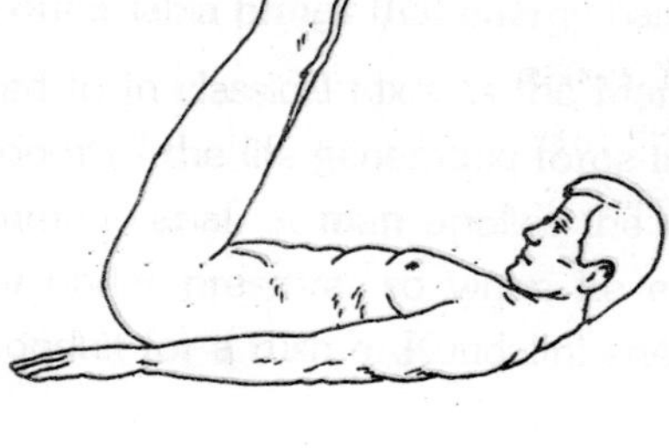

Part C. This exercise is designed to stimulate the sexual energy center into full activity. Eventually you will perform it with the eyes closed so the mind can go within. If you get dizzy at first, keep your eyes open until you become accustomed to the energy rush.

1) Kneel on the floor, hands on the back of the thighs, with the back straight. Tuck the toes under to stimulate the reflex points for the pineal and pituitary glands. Exhale (mouth), press the chin to the chest without bending forward at the waist, and tighten the anus/cervix muscles.
2) While inhaling (nose), lean backward as far as possible, dropping the head back and release the anal sphincter.
3) Return to the starting position and tighten the anus/cervix.
4) Repeat as desired, then do 3 Shiva-Shakti Mudras.

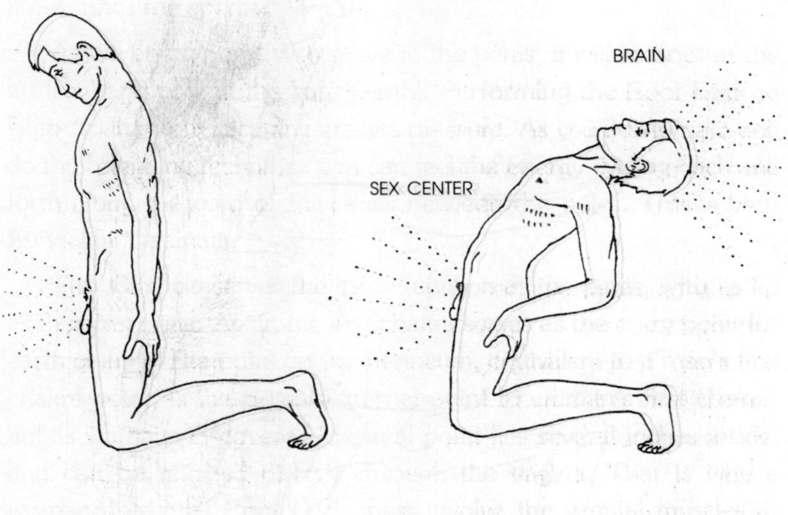

Part D. Although this exercise appears to be difficult, it is really simple and most powerfully stimulates the throat, knees and sex chakras.

1) Sit on the floor, with the legs stretched out in front. Place the hands on the floor beside the hips. The fingers point forward, although some people are more comfortable with fingers pointing to the side or back. Exhale (mouth), tucking the chin onto the chest as you contract the anus/cervix muscle.
2) Inhale (nose), relax the anal/cervix contraction, and lift the hips forward and up as high as possible, so the back is horizontal, like human table. This is accomplished in one upward sweeping motion. The head drops back.
3) Exhale as you return to the starting position.
4) Repeat as desired, then do 3 mudras.

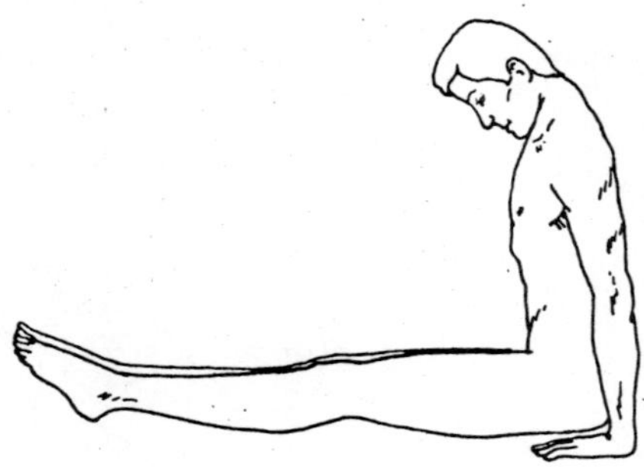

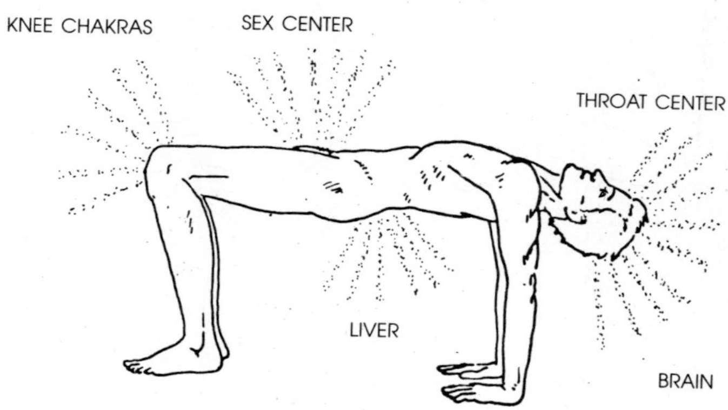

Part E. This exercise stimulates the brain centers, throat center and sex center.

1) Lying on your stomach, place the hands under each shoulder, fingers pointing forward, and push up into the cobra position. The hips are dropped down so the back is arched. The head should be back with the eyes looking up. The weight is supported by the hands and toes. (If you don't have the strength to do this, a modified version would be to rest the body on the floor during the cobra position, or even to work from a hands and knees position until your strength builds.)
2) Exhaling (mouth), bring the hips straight up so the body forms an inverted V. The chin should press onto the chest, with the anus/cervix contracted.
3) Inhale (nose) and relax the anus/cervix, slowly return to the starting position.
4) Repeat as desired, then go directly to Part F.

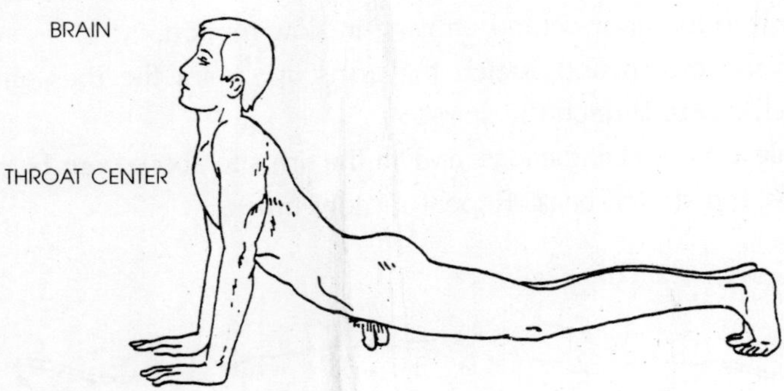

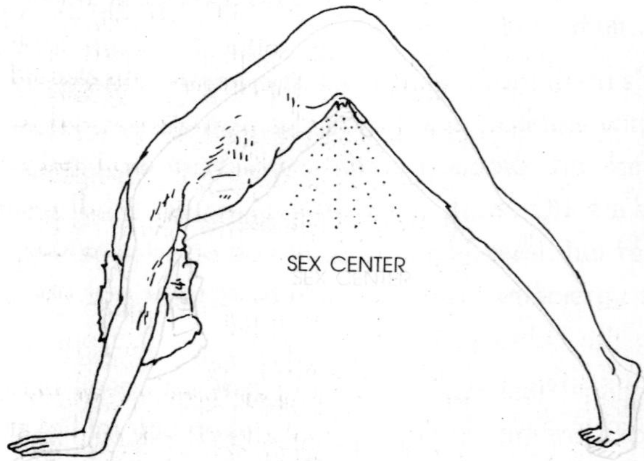

Part F. The final movement is to stretch the spine to allow energy to rise.

1) Lying on your back, inhale as you lift your arms overhead, and stretch to the floor behind, moving in slow motion.
2) Hold the breath and stretch the arms up, point the toes and stretch down. Stretch the spine.
3) Exhale as you relax the legs, and lift the arms to above your face.
4) Inhale and stretch back. Repeat 2 more times.

3. OM-AH-HUM Meditation is the key to getting full benefit from the Rejuvenation postures. After performing the postures, you will have a tremendous amount of sexual energy, much like when you are making love and are highly aroused. You will use breath and mantra to circulate this energy throughout the body, to transmute it to higher levels. If stray thoughts come into your mind, just witness them and then return to being fully present in the moment.

As the postures stimulate and tune up the gross energy system, so the OM-AH-HUM meditation tunes up the finer energy layers of the body for self-healing and increased ability to heal others.

a) Inhale slowly. Hold the breath.

b) Exhale while intoning the mantra OM-AH-HUM. Experience "OM" in the forehead, feel "AH" in the throat, and "HÙM" in the sex center. To drive that sound more intensely into the sex center, tense the anus/cervix muscle as you say "HUM." Then relax, inhale, and send the sex energy to the brain for transmutation into spiritual light.

c) Perform 3 times aloud, then internalize.

d) Sit in silence for 10 minutes and experience the energy expanding in your body and brain. Notice any thoughts that might drift through your mind. Just watch them come and go as a detached observer.

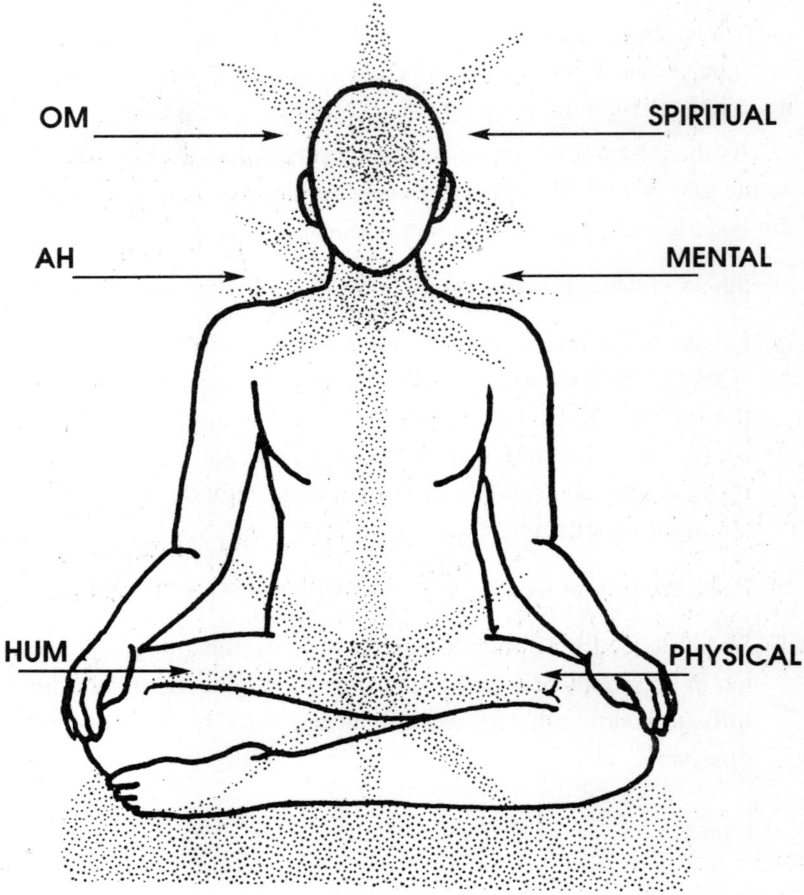
OM
SPIRITUAL
AH
MENTAL
HUM
PHYSICAL

Couple Practice

Chakra Charging Massage.

This is the second half of the Kundalini Massage (page 104). It brings the energy back into the body to prepare for making love. This form of massage works on the etheric level. The one giving the massage is projecting psychic energy through the palms of the hands to stimulate the chakras of the one receiving. This may seem abstract, but the one receiving has no doubt that something is happening.

If you have just done the Rejuvenation exercises you will have an abundance of energy to give. Now bring the energy into your hands as we did preparing for the Kundalini Massage . Let this be a meditation for both of you. Be totally engrossed in the experience. Become ever more sensitive to the subtle currents you are working with.

This is not a rigid formula, just a starting point. Trust your intuition. If you are drawn to spend a lot of time in a given area, and less time somewhere else, trust that.

You can use this time to practice "reading" a body, as in Lesson One. Notice the texture of the energy at each chakra. Be available for any information that presents itself to you. The quieter your mind is, the more available you are to receive communications psychically. Use the techniques in Lesson Eight to quiet your mind.

The massage is described as if a man were giving, a woman receiving. The same steps apply when positions are reversed.

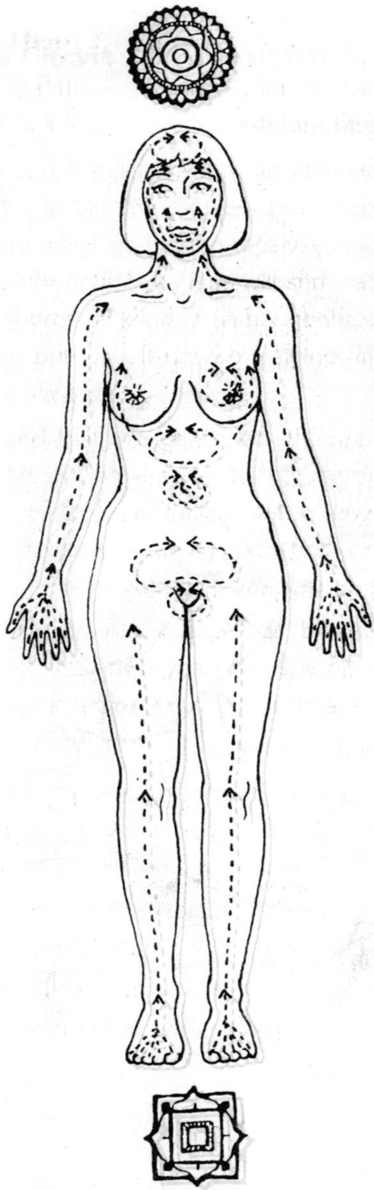

TANTRIC CHARGING TECHNIQUE

1) **Feet Chakras.** Begin where earth energy enters the body. Hold the feet and feel a connection with them.
2) **Legs.** Sweep up the legs, following the lines of the meridians. Stroking the outside of her legs stimulates her Shiva energy and relaxes the uro-genital system. Stroking the inner legs awakens her Shakti, stimulating the sexual nadis connected to the vagina, to start her secretions flowing.
3) **Sex Center.** Project psychic heat through your palm over her pubic area. This electrifies the vaginal fluids and creates the hormones which are activated by ojas. Make small circular movements.
4) **Solar Plexus Center.** The energy of the ojas is then collected into the solar plexus, the reservoir of psychic energy, to create a living dynamo of energy.
5) **Heart Center.** Now pull the energy up the breastbone, massaging the thymus gland to open her heart chakra. This directly stimulates the immune system, protecting her against disease.
6) **Breasts.** Sweep the energy up the sides of the breasts several times. Then place the palms over the nipples and make tiny circles. Massaging her breasts in this way, while projecting energy through your palm chakra, signals to the female genetic code a false pregnancy, the presence of new life in the reproductive organs. In response, her body will relax the flow of menstrual blood, just as if the sucking of an infant were inhibiting normal menstrual cycle.
7) **Throat Center**. Project energy to the thyroid gland, the regulator of metabolism.
8) **Arms.** Sweep the energy from her hands up her arms, shoulders, neck and head and out.
9) **Third Eye.** Place the palm of your sending hand over her forehead to energize the psychic center.
10) **Balancing.** With one hand at her head and the other above her vagina, feel the cool energy at her head.This shows that the Shakti energy has been transmuted all the way up her spine.
11) **Grounding.** To bring the Shakti energy back into the body, make sweeping strokes down both sides of the body, from head to foot, following the body contours. The final stroke would come directly down the front center line.

Awareness

Your Belief System. Bring into consciousness your attitudes about aging. Do you have a resistance to the idea that rejuvenation is possible? Are you convinced that aging is inevitable and not to be interfered with? Do you question whether that's something you even want? Or do you look forward to being old and infirm so no one will expect much from you? Do you expect to be sexually active all your life, or do you have a built-in age limit when sexual activity is no longer part of your life?

The attitudes and expectations you hold, even if you are not conscious of them, strongly affect the way your body sustains itself. At least know what those attitudes are.

Lesson 8

Meditation and Mantra

Mantras are transcendental sounds of power which produce a specific reaction within the human body and mind. Mantras are certain qualities of vibration from the ethers, first heard by pure beings so deep in meditation that they merged with the inner light. Those same vibrations can be used by others to open into higher states of consciousness and awaken their dormant psychic powers. Mantras create a resonance between you and your inner depths.

It is the sound, not the meaning of the words, that has power. Translated to another language they have no effect. Some westernized tantric texts tell you to chant words like "love" as if that would affect your experience. They miss the point of the mantra.

Many famous mantras are the names of deities in the Hindu pantheon. We have had students pull away from using these words for fear they were compromising their integrity by invoking heathen gods! Realize that the mantra evokes a certain aspect of being. Each god was created to personify some aspect. It's not surprising that the gods would be named after the mantra, not the other way around.

Constant repetition of these sounds tunes out other stimuli, resulting in withdrawal of the senses from the outer world, allowing you to tune to the inner world. The nervous system, usually in a frantic race to relay incoming information, becomes very still with no messages to process. You then become conscious with no thoughts to be conscious of, conscious of more and more subtle energies around you, until finally you become conscious of your at-one-ment with the Universe. That is liberation, the goal of all yogas.

The practice of mantra repetition is called Japa Yoga, one of the most ancient and safest paths. It is effective because it is mechanical. Since self-awareness is simply a matter of perception, and perception is a mechanical process, all you need to do is fine-tune the machinery. The problem is, it takes many hours, every day for many years to make any progress. Not many in the West have that much patience or dedication. Also, you must use the mantra that is specifically suited to your personality and only a master can tell you what it is.

The use of mantras is very important in Tantric Kriya Yoga, but, as usual, Tantra has come up with faster ways to get results. The mantras we use are universal, so anyone can use them effectively.

OM is the cosmic seed mantra, the sound of enlightenment. The OM mantra centers one's thoughts and is good preparation for meditation. It brings relaxation and a sense of peace within. OM is useful for getting in touch with the higher mind or higher Self.

One of the keys to using the mantra effectively is correct pronunciation. It has to vibrate properly or there is no energy. There are many ways to chant the OM mantra, each one vibrating on a different level, producing different effects in different chakras. If you want to activate the brain chakras, intone OH only briefly, then go quickly into the MMM sound which is carried for the remainder of the breath. You can feel the vibration in the Third Eye.

The EE mantra is useful for activating the Sixth Chakra and quieting the mind. Use a high pitch to intone this mantra, one that vibrates the medulla oblongata (the spot where the brain and spinal column meet), the back portal to the Third Eye, its feminine aspect.

Mantras used in the tantric rituals and initiation include:

OM NAMA SHIVAYA - an invocation of the solar (Shiva) energy.

OM SHIVA HUM - invokes the consciousness of Shiva to prepare for his union with Shakti. HUM is the sound of power. It forces an energy into realization.

OM MANE PADME HUM - enlightenment made manifest as male enters female, the Jewel in the Lotus. Chant this mantra 5-10 minutes, alone or with your mate, to create an exquisite space.

GATE,GATE, PARAGATE PARASAMGATE, BODHI SWAHA. From the Tibetan Heart Sutra, this lovely mantra allows energy fields to touch, to merge, so that the isolated individual feels at one with another person, or with a group. To stimulate the heart chakra, feel the vibration of the "AH" sounds in the chest.

Mantras can be used for healing. The Bija Mantras (Lesson Six) have a healing influence on any ailment near their corresponding chakra. Advanced mantras will be given as you move through levels of the Cobra Breath.

To Practice the Mantras, sit in a relaxed meditative pose, either on the floor or on a chair. Let your mind be relaxed as you chant. Don't force concentration, just let it happen. Take a deep breath through the nose. As the breath is released, the mantra is pronounced, clearly and steadily, resounding until the breath is spent. Then inhale again and repeat the mantra. Continue until you feel the effects of the mantra or until you wish to stop.

One secret for using a mantra is to decrease the volume with each repetition until you are able to internalize it, that is, to hear it in your mind. The mantra starts as a sound vibration, but as it becomes internalized it really generates power. To chant at the same volume has less effect.

Another secret, said to be one of the Great Secrets of Power, was only recently revealed by the great Yogis of the Himalayas. When using a mantra to activate a certain chakra, pronounce the mantra silently as you inhale and audibly as you exhale. The silent mantra creates a vibration in the etheric body, the voiced mantra draws power from Kundalini to make manifest that etheric vibration, releasing the power of the chakra.

Khechari Mudra technique is another secret for using mantras, which other systems fail to tell you. A mantra can take you into an altered state of consciousness, but if you wish to use a mantra in your daily life, keep your tongue touching the roof of your mouth. Roll the tongue tip back as far as possible without straining.

Using a mantra will keep you serene, as long as you remember to contain the energy. Khechari Mudra activates the anal sphincter muscle and keeps your energy from being released and depleted so the vibration wells up in you and keeps you focused and energized. By activating the anal sphincter, Khechari Mudra helps to stimulate and awaken Kundalini Shakti.

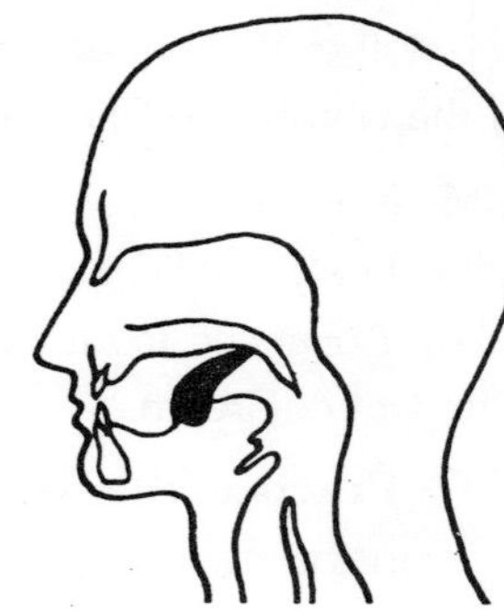

Khechari mudra is helpful in quieting the mind. As the mind chatters, your tongue says the words silently in micro-movements. Immobilizing the tongue stops the chatter.

To stick your tongue back in your throat is considered in the Hindu tradition to be the worship of Ganesh, the elephant God. The tongue symbolizes the penis, so you are making love to yourself.

There are pressure points and glands in the palate which control many functions of the body. Khechari Mudra is very beneficial to health. The practice creates a pressure at the back of the throat that stimulates the medulla. The medulla oblongata is one of the master points in acupressure. (It is said that this is where the Breath of God enters the body.) Stimulating this point gives the body an all-over energy boost. As you release the tongue you will feel a vibration at the back of your neck that produces a wave of relaxation.

The tip of the tongue is the end of the energy channel, and so it is a switch, a control mechanism. In opening the third eye, the psychic bridge must be joined, that is, a direct connection from the medulla to the Ajna Center. The tongue tip, touching the roof of the mouth, in the hollow about an inch behind the teeth, completes that connection and stimulates the pituitary. When the tongue touches the roof of the mouth, it stimulates the crown chakra. When the tongue goes way back so the tip touches the soft palate, it stimulates the pineal gland.

The awakened pineal gland secretes hormones that start dripping down through the system to revitalize your body. When you perfect this practice, you will experience the sweet honey-like taste of "the Divine Nectar" or the "living water." Its taste is most delightful and gives you a feeling of well-being. The nectar includes serotonin, which is the precursor to endorphins, the body's natural propiate. Used together with other practices, Khechari Mudra can produce psychedelic effects.

The nectar removes feelings of hunger and thirst and eventually removes the need to eat. This has been used successfully as a way to lose weight. This practice allows yogis to stay in suspended animation without food or drink for long periods of time.

If, during the exercise, you taste something bitter, that may be harmful, and the practice should be discontinued. It probably means that some chemical, like residual LSD, is stored in the brain.

In the Taoist tradition, the tongue connection is used to complete the Microcosmic orbit of energy. In the Tantra practice it is used primarily to quiet the mind; when you feel the Kundalini energy moving up and down the spine you have a sense of control.

The tongue plays a very crucial part in the tantric experience. When making love, at orgasm we use a certain mantra as we release the Khechari Mudra and the whole body is flooded with energy. This is part of the Cobra Breath Technique.

The effect of Khechari Mudra is enhanced when done in conjunction with a breathing technique called Psychic Breath. Lift the glottis and breathe so it feels like you're breathing through your throat instead of your nose. This produces a gentle snore like the sound of a sleeping baby.

MEDITATION

The true experience of meditation begins when you stop the techniques, release the mantra. Most "meditations" are really forms of self-hypnosis or script-writing that keep the mind agitated and active. When you drop into true meditation, all thoughts cease. The thinker does not exist. There may be images or visions, but no words or concepts; no goals. Tuning into the Universal Mind is cutting off this thinking process of the five senses.

So don't think if you are doing the technique you are doing meditation. I was once under the illusion that chanting OM-OM was meditation. Then I found out that only after I stop chanting OM can I truly hear the OM. Then I am in meditation. Doing the Cobra Breath or any other technique is just preparing you for the state of meditation that is non-thinking; withdrawing the senses; resting in the state of pure blissful consciousness.

HONG SAU MEDITATION

As long as we are in a physical vehicle, operating through ego, we will have thoughts. Meditation practices that claim to still the thoughts are misleading. But there are techniques to stop thought temporarily, just to give us a rest. One of those techniques is the Hong-Sau (pronounced "saw") breath meditation.

The Hong-Sau pranayam is a powerful technique, used to quiet the entire body. Because this technique oxygenates the system, eliminating carbon dioxide, it slows down the activity of the heart and the lungs. When the cardio-vascular system is entirely oxygenated, you don't have to breathe. The breathless state has the effect of quieting the five senses thus allowing a higher state of consciousness to unfold. The body no longer has the need for energy from food and

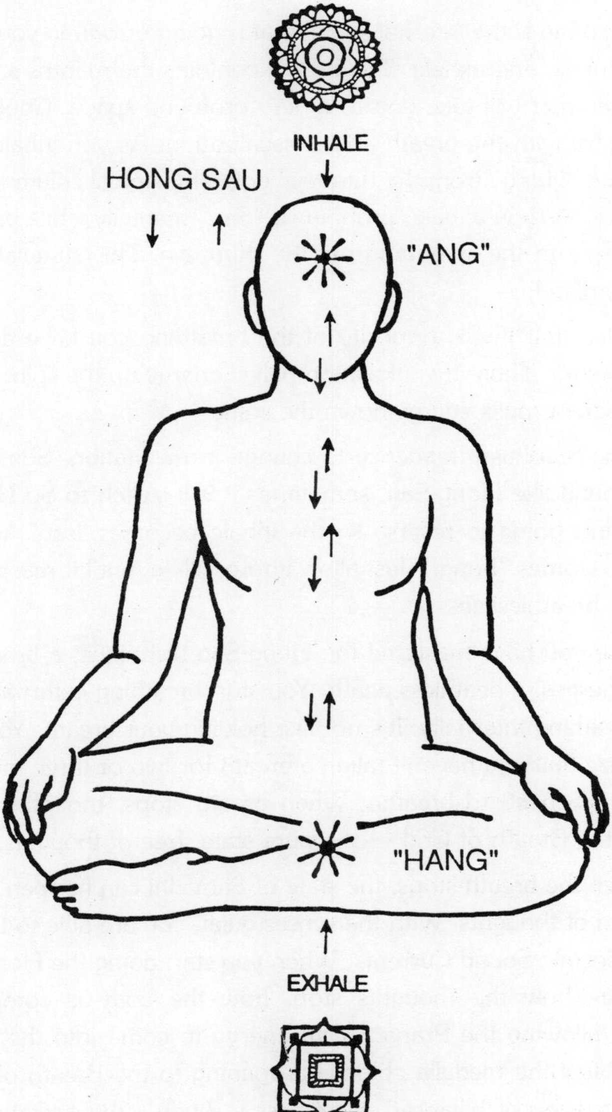
INHALE
HONG SAU
"ANG"
"HANG"
EXHALE

from oxygen for survival. Instead, the body can take sustenance directly from prana that comes into the body through the medulla oblongata.

Hong-Sau is the internal sound that is going on within your body as you inhale and exhale. The breath contains the mantra and that is the key that will take you to a very profound space. Coordinate the mantra with the breath and a visualization. As you inhale, take the sound "Hong" from the third eye down the spinal column to the perineum. As you exhale, pronounce "Sau" mentally while bringing the energy up the spine and out the third eye. This stimulates the pituitary gland.

Notice that this is opposite of the breathing you have done in Prana Mudra. There the inhalation pulled energy up the spine. Here the inhalation pulls energy down the spine.

Hong-Sau has a tendency to change in meditation. Sometimes it will sound like Hong-Sau, sometimes it will switch to So Hum. It might start going in reverse so the inhale becomes "sau" and the exhale becomes "hong." Just allow it to oscillate, until it reaches the point of breathlessness.

Once you have mastered the Hong-Sau technique, a breathless state emerges, a deathless death. You stop breathing externally and start breathing internally. It's not like holding your breath. You simply realize that you haven't taken a breath for two or three minutes, and felt no need to breathe. When breath stops, thoughts stops. That is the Breath of God — the pure state, free of thoughts.

When the breath stops, the state of Samadhi can happen — the cessation of thoughts. With the senses quiet, you are able to tune in to the Cosmic Sound Currents. When you start doing the Hong-Sau you'll see how the thoughts stop, how the body is completely relaxed, allowing the Prana Shakti energy to come into the spine. You will feel the medulla oblongata opening to the Breath of God. This is a state of balanced awareness - Bindu - the twilight zone between waking and sleeping.

After some practice the meditation happens on a mental level, automatically, without you even thinking "Hong-Sau."

Hong-Sau gives you absolute proof that you are not your body. You can see that the breath stops and you are still conscious. What is this consciousness that views the body in suspended animation? Knowing that you exist apart from the body takes away the fear of death.

NOTE: Working with the Hong-Sau mantra makes you feel "spacey." We recommend if you do the Hong-Sau in the morning, especially if you are going out to drive, follow it with the Rejuvenation Postures to reground yourself. Otherwise you may not be able to clearly focus on this reality.

Other Uses of Hong-Sau. The Hong-Sau technique is a very exacting science. That one mantra has been used for thousands of years in many different ways. You can use Hong-Sau for spiritual purposes, or at a sexual level to control climax, as we shall see in the next lesson.

This practice can also produce psychic abilities. When you stop the breath, you can pick up telepathically what another person is thinking. When the breath is calm, the mind is calm and then impressions can be received. If you are receptive the symbols are intelligible and the lessons manifest in your life.

The practice stimulates the nervous system. It cleans out the psychic debris that clogs the nadis, the pranic channels of the body. Over a period of time all the Samskara (attachments to the past) and Vasanas (desires for the future) are removed from the mind. All the hidden fears and neuroses come up for observation. Being the uninvolved witness allows you to release them. And so this process relieves the mind of all its tensions, the source of all physical and mental disease.

The breath mantra will awaken Sushumna, and karma is eliminated symbolically as strange sounds and fantastic experiences arise from your deeper consciousness. This is a purging process.

Hong-Sau Meditation is especially valuable to people who do a great deal of mental work. If you spend too much time in mental processes you get trapped there, and lose the balance between physical and mental. You lose sight of the psychic and spiritual.

A certain symbol appears universally when a student has mastered the Hong-Sau technique. The White Light is the first manifestation. You see a pin-point of light that is your Ajna center, or third eye. The second manifestation is seeing colors, which denote the level of consciousness where you are vibrating. The White Light is one of the most important factors as it starts to move through the body and then expands beyond the body to encompass all, so everything becomes pure White Light. The light overtakes you and you feel you have become the light. This is Samadhi. (If this description reminds you of the description of the Tantric Marriage, it's because that same phenomenon can be brought on by doing Hong Sau Meditation).

There are techniques to activate this vision in a mechanical way, but this is the natural method. This is just to let you know that there is a White Light and that you can receive it. The White Light is a blending of the various colors. Each person will discover his own individual center and that will be the focal point for his meditation.

The Hong-Sau technique has a safety factor. When you get too far out in space, it reels you back in, drops you back into your body. Also it guarantees you that no other entities will enter your body while you are "out." We are all given a certain amount of time to fulfill our Karmic duties before we drop our bodies. Nothing can end your life until that time is complete. You are protected by the cosmos. So you can "die" in meditation and come back with a new level of awareness. St. Paul said "I die daily," and Yogis through history speak of death in this way. Orgasm is referred to as a little death.

Each night when we go to sleep it is as if we die, but each morning we are reborn.

ATTACHMENT

We are dying only to the attachment to objects so pure spirit can flow in. That doesn't mean giving up the object, only the attachment to it, the feeling of having to have it, whether it's pleasure or pain. All forms of desire, whether on the subtle or gross level, become addictive and we must remember there is no permanency on this physical plane. It is "maya," an illusion created by working with the five senses.

Cessation of desires doesn't mean you have to give up anything. Just see where the desire comes from, recognize it for what it is, and if it is appropriate for that moment, enjoy it. Don't cling to a hope of repeating an experience because it will never happen again. Every experience is totally unique.

Once you can make that leap of giving up the attachment you can enjoy anything or anyone you want for that moment, without fear of losing it. The hardest lesson is that of letting go. Everyone on this physical plane in these rented shells is going through that lesson.

By temporarily stopping the thinking process, we stop creating mental vibrations in the ethers. Those vibrations create a manifestation on the physical plane. Hong-Sau is a technique that stops the thinking process, therefore stops the creation of vibrations and the consequences that follow. Eventually you come to that point of balance, Bindu, where you aren't creating more Karma by your desires and attachments.

Our mental computers run all the time. We are all on overload, and all we have to think about are thoughts. That is not healthy. We need time to shut down the system, to let the system repair itself. We must let go of thinking the thoughts and become the thoughts.

To connect into the Universal Mind you must cut off this thinking process, and "die" on this physical plane. Then Universal Mind comes through. By shutting down the system you allow the body to repair itself, allow mind to connect with its source. When mind and body are in tune, spirit automatically comes in. Hong Sau is the carrier wave which gives you awareness of Atman, the Universal Soul, via the five senses.

Individual Practice

Your daily meditation routine should now include the following:

1. **Rishi Isometrics** 3 times each
2. **Complete Breath** 7 times
3. **Nadi Soghana** 7 times
4. **OM and EE mantra** 3 times each (Omit if you get spacey.)
5. **Hong Sau Meditation** (10 minutes)

   a) Sit in a meditative posture. Perform Khechari Mudra (without the Psychic Breath), breathing always through the nose. Follow the breath in and out. As you inhale, picture the breath's energy coming in through the Third Eye, traveling down the spinal column. At the end of the inhalation, contract the anus/cervix and then release the contraction. As you exhale, picture the energy traveling up the spine, through the medulla oblongata and out of the third eye, projecting 2-3 inches.

   b) Add to this visualization the breath mantra, Hong-Sau. As you inhale, mentally chant the mantra "Hong." As you exhale, mentally chant the mantra "Sau" (pronounced "saw"). As thoughts and feelings enter your mind, watch them come and go as a detached observer. When material emerges from the subconscious as symbols, memories, or feelings, again be the observer.

   c) Continue for ten or fifteen minutes or for as long as you are comfortable. At some point you should no longer feel the need to breathe.
6. **Wait 15 minutes** before showering. Wait 30 minutes before eating.

Couple Practice

1. The Individual Practice Can Be Done With Your Partner. Perform the Rishi Isometrics, as described in Lesson 3, maintaining eye contact. Do the Hong Sau Meditation back to back, synchronizing the breath in both bodies, extending your awareness to include your partner's breath and body.

2. Hong Sau Is a Delay Technique. While making love, when you feel orgasm approaching, start the Hong Sau to relax your body and diffuse the energy. Then build to a higher orgasmic level.

Awareness

1. Become Aware of the Chatter in your head all the waking day. Occasionally step back from it and become the Witness. You will be tempted to judge yourself for being so chattery, especially compared to the lovely silence of Hong Sau Meditation. Don't allow judgement to enter in. <u>The Witness is uninvolved, non-judgemental. That is the key.</u>

Know that this endless monologue is keeping you isolated, is the barrier to experiencing God directly every moment of your life. Realize that you are creating that barrier moment by moment. Is that really what you want?

a) Notice how much of the chatter is devoted to self-justification - about how you were right in your actions and the other fellow was wrong.
b) Observe how much the chatter repeats itself - like hearing a record over and over.
c) See how much it dwells on the past and holds you in situations that don't exist any more.
d) See how much it dwells on the future, anticipating problems and satisfactions that will probably never materialize.
e) Notice yourself rehearsing what you will say (in the future) to someone who misused you (in the past). This keeps you out of the present.
f) When you are in the present, your mind is quiet. How often does that happen?

2. Bring Into Consciousness the Attachments that hold you bound. The story is told of a spiritual seeker who came to the master asking how he could free himself from his attachments. The master jumped up and wrapped his arms around a tree trunk. Clutching the tree, he began to wail "How can I make this tree let go of me?" The student left, embarrassed but wiser.

Imagine that you were in the presence of a radiant master who told you that you were very close to self-realization. All that was left was to let go of one thing. What is the one thing that would be hardest to give up?

- Position: Status in the community, your profession, or your family.
- Achievement: The sense of having accomplished something special, or needing to.
- Possessions: Things you now have and couldn't live without, used to have and resent losing, or intend to have at some point.
- Resentments: Unwillingness to forgive and forget.
- Sense of inadequacy: Feeling incompetent, unworthy, guilty.
- Willfulness: Always being right; Having the last word; Having it your way.
- Feeling superior to "ordinary" people, in a class by yourself.
- Nameless fears; expecting the worst; being the victim.

Search your heart and see what games you are clinging to.

Lesson 9

Generating and Transmuting Sexual Energy

In this lesson you will learn 1) Sexual activators to loosen and arouse the body; 2) Energy locks to control the flow of energy; 3) Mudras to generate intense sexual energy; 4) Masturbation as a tantric practice; 5) Techniques to transmute the sexual energy up the spine on the breath; and 6) How to transform the essence of the seminal and ovarian fluid, using that prana to charge the blood.

SEXUAL KRIYA ACTIVATORS

This exercise routine (demonstrated on the video) is designed to dramatically stimulate sexual energy. Find some music to move to, either sensuous, belly-dance music, primal drums or something really "hot."

Tummy Rub. Two minutes each day spent rubbing circles on your tummy will build a reservoir of energy in your solar plexus; your digestion and elimination will improve and your weight will normalize. Make a spiral around the navel, small circles, getting larger, and then back to smaller. First up on the right, down on the left for a minute; then reverse direction.

Shakeout. To release held tension and make that energy available for action, to stimulate every energy corridor in the physical and etheric body, full-body shaking is most effective. You could easily go on fifteen minutes. Involuntary shaking is one manifestation of Shakti energy. If you really let yourself go, the shaking will take over and you will be shaken. Surrendering to the energy is a prerequisite for full orgasm.

Head and Shoulder Rolls. You will soon be pulling a lot of energy up into the brain. Make sure there is no blockage from muscle tension in the neck and shoulders. Slowly roll the head twice, then the other direction twice. Lift the shoulders and roll forward, and repeat. Lift the shoulders and roll backward and repeat.

Pelvic Thrusts. This movement is essential to the sexual act, and is also a primary way to generate sexual energy. All men do the movement, but "American style" for only a minute or two. Extended lovemaking requires more stamina. Since there is no other activity (except erotic dancing) that includes this movement, it must be practiced.

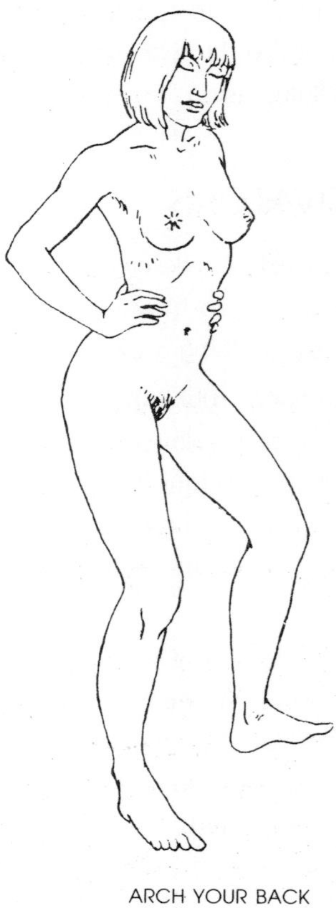

ARCH YOUR BACK

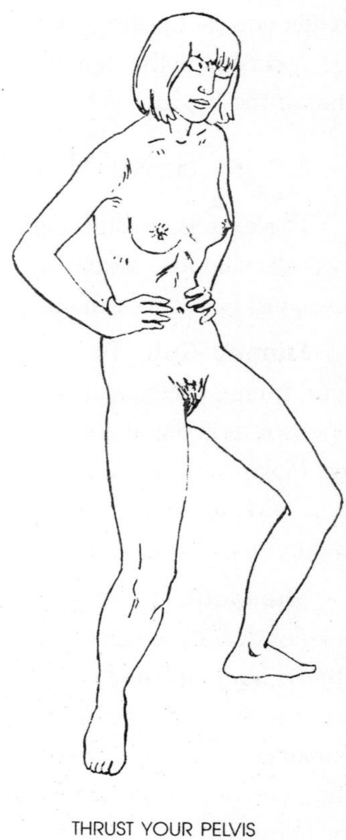

THRUST YOUR PELVIS

Take care to hold the rib cage stationary so the movement only involves the pelvic bowl. Few people can actually move the pelvis independently. For almost everyone it is frozen. Watch yourself in a mirror to make sure your rib cage is not moving. By such movement, a woman can provide herself clitoral stimulation. Any woman who doesn't make these movements while she is making love is denying herself the fulness of pleasure. Even without a partner, doing the movements is arousing.

b) When you have mastered the movement, give it extra intensity by coordinating the thrusts with the breath. Thrust forward as you exhale through the mouth, arch backward as you inhale through the nose.

c) Adding root contractions gives you a supercharge of energy. As you thrust forward, contract the anus/cervix. As you arch back, relax the anus/cervix.

d) Add arm movements to enhance the breathing and involve the whole body. As you thrust forward, pull the arms strongly back. Work the arms in opposition to the pelvis to maintain your balance.

Pelvic Circles. When the spine is more flexible and the pelvic muscles are looser, more energy can flow in the sexual process. Imagine you are drawing a large circle with your genitals. Hold your hands on your hips as a reminder not to move your rib cage.

Making these movements while making love adds variety and increases stimulation. When both partners move in this way (in opposite directions) every part of the vagina and penis receive stimulation.

Nipple Circles. Use the open hand (palm chakra) to stimulate your nipples while you move your hips. This is arousing and therefore generates hormones.

A Taoist exercise for women (The Deer) uses circles on the breasts to lessen, or even stop, the loss of blood through menstrual flow. The added stimulation to the breasts is a deterent to breast cancer, and even changes the size of the breasts. Just stroke the breasts, not the nipples, with circular motions, both hands stroking up the center, around, and down the outside. Continue for 36 strokes. Reverse direction for another 36 strokes. Outward circles increase breast size, inward circles decrease the size.

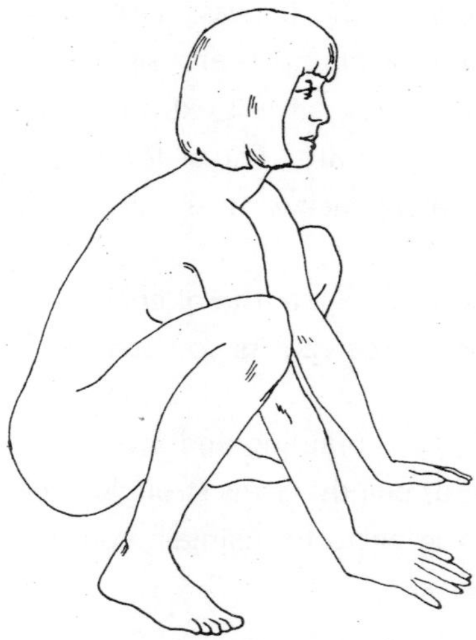

Narrow Squat. Orientals spend much of their life in a squat position. Westerners need to stretch out tight muscles to allow more energy to flow into the sexual organs. Place feet shoulder width apart, squat with arms inside knees. This is a great position to practice anal contractions since it puts pressure on the lower end of Ida and Pingala channels, near their junction at the first chakra.

Wide Squat. With feet twice shoulder width apart you get a better stretch. Begin thrusting the pelvis in this position. Add the anal contractions. Thrust and contract, back and relax. This is guaranteed to give you an energy rush as you put pressure on the sacrum so the current of energy is starting to build.

Cat Stretches. Assume a hands and knees position. Arch your back like an angry cat and then collapse it like a sway-back horse. Move the head opposite from the spine. While lifting the spine, you drop the head. While lowering the spine, you lift the head. Add the breathing and the anal/cerical contractions, just as with Pelvic Thrusts. When the pevis moves forward, exhale and contract. When it moves back, inhale and relax. This stimulates the sexual glands while it limbers up the spine. This movement is particularly effective for women who suffer menstrual distress.

Butterfly. Sit with soles of feet touching and bounce the knees to stretch out the inner thigh.

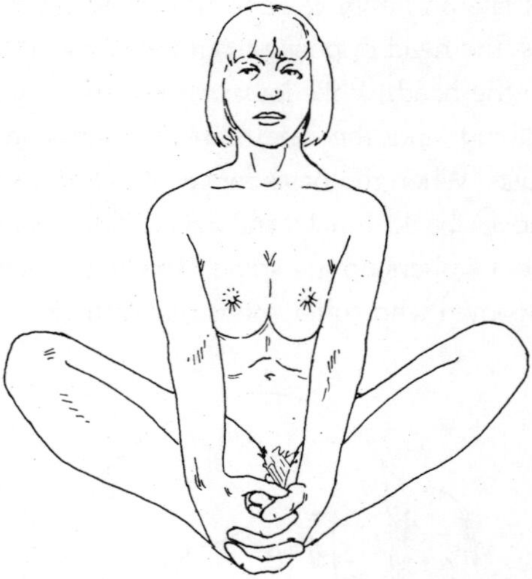

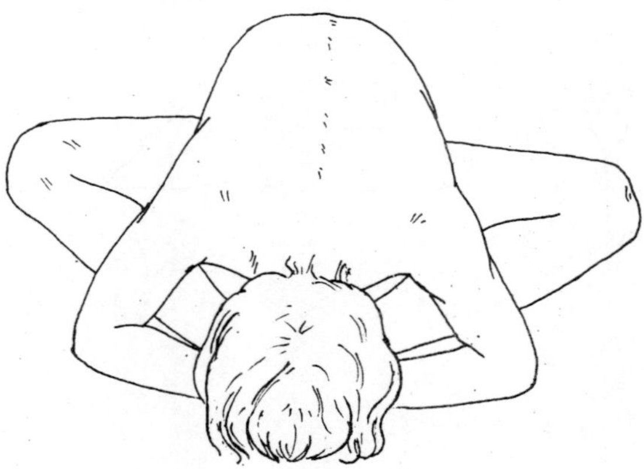

Collapse Forward. From the butterfly position, grab your feet and pull your head down towards the feet. This provides a stretch for the lower spine to allow Kundalini to rise unimpeded.

PREPARING THE ENERGY PUMP

Those who are new to tantric studies may not be in touch with the lower part of their bodies. Let's become acquainted with the muscles that are used in the techniques to follow.

To locate these muscles:

- Squeeze your buttocks (gluteus muscles) together, as if trying to hold a pencil.
- Locate your anus mentally.
- Touch your tongue to the roof of your mouth as far back as possible and feel the anus respond.
- Contract the anus, as if stopping a bowel movement.
- Feel the contraction spread forward to the genitals which will probably twitch. (In orgasm these muscles all twitch.)
- Contract the muscle that would stop urine flow.

You are learning to stimulate the base center, which in turn stimulates the nearby Kundalini egg. The Kunda Gland referred to in classical yogic texts, is tucked just under the sacrum, a mystery to anatomists who don't know what it does. All the ancient mystical references can be understood in terms of the physical body.

For men, locate with your fingers the area between the testicles and the anus. Anatomically it's called the perineum. Esoterically it's the external stimulation point for the base chakra. When you press that spot you produce a bandha or energy lock.

The female base chakra is high in the vagina, on the posterior wall, about 1" from the cervix. Stimulating it directly should be done carefully since it is very sensitive, but it can be stimulated indirectly by touching the G-Spot, a small area on the front wall of the vagina, one to two inches inside.

One of the devices used in the tantric temples in India to stimulate the base chakra involves sitting on a wooden ball the size of a golf ball. For the Western world we start more gently. Fold a towel into a very small volume. Sit on the towel in any comfortable position, even on a chair.

Men sit so that pressure is put on the spot between the genitals and the anus. Make sure the testicles are hanging free. This pressure cuts off the passage of the seminal fluid into the bladder. It's important in doing the auto-erotic meditation that you stop this flow since you can't discharge the fluid.

For women, adjust the towel so it puts pressure on your clitoris. This stimulates the second chakra, but also involves the root.

With this pressure on Muladhara, do anal contractions. See if you can feel a slight pressure coming back down on the towel. If not, adjust your body so more pressure is applied. The classical way to do this is to sit on your heel. If that is comfortable, create the pressure that way. Continue to contract and relax very rapidly. See if you feel some sensations in your genitals.

The purpose of Tantra is to attune us so sensitively to our bodies that we can feel the movement of subtle energy through the meridians and nadis. The most sensitive area of our bodies is the genitals. Once we are in tune with those sensations we no longer need the towel or golf ball. Those are just learning devices.

BANDHAS: THE ENERGY LOCKS

The human body has three natural locks that control the movement of pranic energy:

Chin Lock - Jalandhara Bandha

Diaphragm Lock - Uddiyana Bandha

Root Lock - Moola Bandha

When these three have been mastered individually they can be done simultaneously:

Triple Lock - Maha Bandha

As we inhale we bring Prana into the body to be stored in the energy reservoir at Manipura chakra. Prana consists of five different energies. One of those, called Apana, normally moves downward in the body and is eliminated with excretions, escaping back to the earth. The Root Lock blocks its discharge and reverses its direction so you can conserve this energy and direct it back up to rejoin Prana at Manipura.

It is important to maintain a balance of Prana and Apana. If the Apana has drained out, the Prana can be pulled down into the vacuum and also lost through the anus. When the energy drain is stopped with the Root Lock, the Apana builds up in the lower torso. This earth energy rises to meet the pranic energy in Manipura. When there is enough pressure, the combined energies rush to the base center and start to ascend Sushumna. The rejoining of these energies triggers a flow of Kundalini up the spine.

The Diaphragm Lock, like a lock in a canal, then encourages the energy to rise up Sushumna. Capping this increased energy with the Chin Lock creates a metaphysical hydraulic pressure in the energy body so, when you take the Cobra Breath, the Prana Shakti is pushed up the spine into the Spiritual centers, opening you up chakra by chakra, propelling you into higher levels of consciousness.

Chin Lock.

1) Sit in the easy pose, knees touching the floor if possible, with palms on knees. Relax and close your eyes. Keep your attention on the throat chakra.
2) Inhale deeply and hold the breath. Move the head back (like a Balinese dancer, head stays vertical) and drop your chin a little. Straighten your arms and lock the elbows, pulling shoulders up and forward. Hold as long as is comfortable.
3) Raise the head, relax the body and exhale. (Don't try to exhale before you release the chin lock or you will hurt yourself).
4) Repeat, after breath has returned to normal, up to 10 repetitions.

This is a valuable preparation for meditation as it slows the heart rate, calms the mind and relieves stress. It also massages and stimulates the thyroid which affects many functions of the body, including sexual functions. This is another way to work with the throat chakra if communication is a problem for you.

CAUTION: Anyone subject to strokes, high blood pressure or heart problems should not do this practice.

Diaphragm Lock.

1) Sit in the easy pose, knees touching the floor if possible, with palms on knees. Relax and close your eyes. Keep your attention on navel chakra.
2) Exhale deeply. Perform a chin lock (Hold the breath, move the head back, drop the chin. Straighten your arms and lock the elbows, pulling shoulders up and forward.)
3) Contract abdominal muscles upward and inward. Hold as long as comfortable.
4) Relax muscles, raise head and then inhale.
5) When breathing is back to normal, you can repeat up to 10 times.

As you draw the diaphragm up and press the abdominal organs back, you massage and tone the liver, pancreas, kidneys, spleen, stomach and adrenals. This stimulation improves their performance and does wonders for any ailments of these organs (constipation, indigestion, worms, diabetes, etc.). The stimulation to Manipura, the prana reservoir, enhances distribution of prana through the body, particularly up the spinal canal.

CAUTION: Practice only on an empty stomach. This is not for people with ulcers or pregnancy. Cautions for chin lock also apply.

Root Lock.

1) Sit in an easy pose, ideally with your perineum or clitoris pressing on your heel, palms upon thighs. Move your attention to the base center.

2) Inhale deeply. Perform chin lock. (Hold the breath, move the head back, drop the chin. Straighten your arms and lock the elbows, pulling shoulders up and forward.)
3) Contract the anus (cervix for women). Press down and forward on the floor until you feel a twitch in the vagina or a pull in the testicles. Hold for as long is comfortable.
4) Release the contraction and chin lock, take a sniff of air, and exhale. Feel sexual energy rising from the base center to the brain (or to the heart or whatever body part needs energy).

Performing the root lock provides a daily massage of the urogenital system. Peristalsis is stimulated so constipation is removed. The anus is strengthened and piles removed. Sexual glands are massaged, which will stimulate the release of vital hormones. A primary concern in Tantra is maintaining the sexual glands in optimum tone, since they are the master glands which energize the other systems of the body. Sexual hormones are the essence of Kundalini and the key to rejuvenation.

As you contract the anal sphincter muscle and block the Apana escape, the energy begins to build up. You will experience a very pleasant tingling sensation in your genitals.

Triple Lock.

1) Sit in an easy pose in Gyana Mudra (thumbs and index fingers touching). Shiva sit with your anus on your left heel, Shakti with your yoni on your left heel. Put the sole of your right foot against your left knee.
2) Inhale to the count of seven. Exhale to the count of nine.
3) Hold the breath out, pull the abdomen up and in, move the head back, drop the chin, and tighten your anus. Hold for the count of sixteen.
4) Relax — inhale and exhale very slowly three times.
5) Repeat complete technique for a total of seven times.

SEX ENERGY GENERATORS

Once you have mastered the energy locks you are ready to incorporate them into more complicated techniques that are the core of tantric practice: Aswini Mudra and Vajroli Mudra.

These practices both generate intense energy in the lower body while keeping it contained. This builds up pressure in the energy channels. Once the containment is released, that pressurized energy shoots up the spine, breaking through any blocks or restrictions.

Aswini Mudra (gesture of the horse) — An ancient system of massage consisting of dynamic contractions of the anal sphincter muscle which spread forward into the genitals (high in the vagina for women). This is a very powerful technique to pump the energy up into Manipura. The contractions are mild, but rapid.

1) Sit on your heel or on a rolled up towel or tennis ball so pressure is felt on Muladhara Chakra (between genitals and anus for men, on clitoris for women).
2) Fill the lungs about 1/3 full. Contract and relax the anus 20 times, about twice per second.
3) Continue inhaling another 1/3. Contract and relax 20 more times.
4) Inhale the last 1/3. Contract and relax the last 20 times.
5) Hold the breath, pull the shoulders forward and press the chin against the chest for a moment. Feel the heat and hydraulic pressure build up.
6) Take a sniff of air and exhale through the nose as you release the tension. Feel an energy flush through the entire body. Visualize the energy moving up the spine.

Vajroli Mudra (the thunderbolt) stimulates the genitals with prana activated blood. It is a wonderful way to tighten vaginal walls which were stretched out during childbirth. Having a "tighter fit" means much more stimulation, and more pleasure, for both partners during intercourse. For most men this exercise is <u>the</u> solution to the problem of premature ejaculation. In many cases it also resolves impotency. Mastery of this exercise allows you to experience longer and more intense orgasm. When you are able to do this for fifteen minutes you can have a fifteen minute orgasm.

1) Sit in an easy pose, palms upon thighs. Close your eyes and relax.
2) Move your attention to the sex center: Men — base of penis; Women — below the clitoris.
3) Inhale through the nose as you pull energy up the spine. Swallow and retain the breath at the Third Eye. Pull up the sexual organs by contracting the muscle you would use to stop the flow of urine and the lower abdomen muscles.
4) Continue to hold the breath as you relax and contract ten times.
5) On the tenth relaxation, exhale through the nose and experience sexual energy rising from the sex center to the brain (or whatever body part needs energy).
6) A man can make these muscles even stronger by adding more weight. Place a washcloth over the penis and lift that. Then make it a wet washcloth, which is heavier. Masters of this practice are said to be able to lift 150 pounds with their genitals. But don't try that without expert supervision.

Vajroli Mudra exercises the genitals, particularly the muscles used to stop urine flow. Dr. Kegel discovered the power of the PC (pubococcygeus) muscle exercises and they have become a standard tool in this country in preparing for childbirth and overcoming sexual disfunction. The tantric masters had been doing "Kegels" for thousands of years, but much more effectively.

The secret to making any process more powerful is to coordinate it with the breath and control of the etheric energy. This mudra strongly affects the nadis that supply the sex organs with psychic energy. After some practice a man can retain the energy from the semen even when ejaculating. That energy can be used for his health and spiritual growth instead of being wasted.

CREATIVE MASTURBATION

Masturbation can be a tantric meditation, a springboard into spiritual awakening. It can be a healing process, a way to resolve personal and business problems, by turning off the conscious mind and letting the unconscious do the work. It allows you to "get into" your body and out of your head.

We must learn to be in tune with our bodies. Unfortunately in this culture we learn very early to be ashamed of our bodies. We learn from our parents, as they learned from their parents, that it is not nice to touch your genitals. Everyone does it anyway, but with a sense of shame, in a secretive unconscious way.

As recently as twenty years ago authorities were still saying that if you masturbated you would go blind or insane. They were ignorant of the energy masturbation makes available to you if used properly. True, too much ejaculation depletes your reserve of energy. That's why in Tantra we ask you not to ejaculate, or, for a woman, not to climax, until you have transmuted the energy.

According to research, the most intense orgasm is produced by masturbation, either by yourself or mutual masturbation by partners (which is an important part of foreplay).

While you are learning to do the Creative Masturbation technique you might need imagery. Feel free to indulge in as much fantasy as you need to start the energy. This energy goes into the central nervous system, which doesn't care where the stimulus came from. So whatever turns you on is right for you. The degree of excitement is what counts, not the method of obtaining it.

Aswini Mudra, contracting the anal sphincter, creates a heat which you can physically feel. Do this before masturbating to generate even more energy.

Masturbate to a point just short of orgasm. When the energy is at its peak, concentrate on the in-breath and draw the energy up the spinal column to the point where you want it — to the solar plexus if your energy reserve is low, to the heart if your are guarded there, to the third eye if you wish to go into an abstract spiritual space.

Another technique is to sit back to back with your partner masturbating together and then bringing the energy up the spine. You can feel the pulsation of the energy shooting up the spine with the breath.

We can control the movement of energy because we reinforce the visualization with the breath. This is an experiment you do two or three times just to see if your can manipulate the energy. Then you make love, because the energy has to go somewhere. If you don't release it, it will cause problems in the internal organs. Some schools prohibit you from releasing in orgasm. We don't think that is a healthy or wise practice until you have fully mastered the art of transmuting energy.

In the 1800s the Oenida Society practiced Karezza where there was a lot of foreplay but no climax, which was supposed to "magnetize" the body. While the members enjoyed a warm glow during the lovemaking, they often discovered within two weeks that inflammation had set into the pelvic area. When you are aroused and the blood is not released, it takes many days for it to dissipate. After you do the masturbation, be sure to pull that energy up.

This process is effortless. There is no trying. Just be aware of the energy going up. There is a bit of visualization, but more a matter of becoming conscious of the energy which is already there, especially if you have done the Aswini Mudra. Touching the genitals simply aids you in feeling this intense energy. You are internalizing that outside energy that comes from manual manipulation.

In Vama Marga (left-hand path) we are taught to utilize sexual energy with a partner. When you have mastered the direction of your energy in masturbation, you can perform the transmuting process with a partner. That brings in a whole new dimension of energy.

TRANSMUTING ENERGY

The normal person is exhausted after sex, ready to sleep. Many use sex or masturbation to put themselves to sleep at night. That is sex at the animal level. After learning to harness this energy, you become vibrant and have more energy than you know what to do with. People turn as you go by, wondering what makes you so attractive. Transmuting an orgasm is a great way to raise your energy in the morning!

Tantric sex is taking lust out of love. You start with lust. Start where you are. When you learn how to transmute this energy, it turns into spiritual energy. When you learn to use this energy, you will have mystical experiences. The Tantra system allows you to go out into the cosmos and then come back to operate on the physical plane too. You learn how to recirculate this energy in the body.

We will learn to transform the essence of the seminal and ovarian fluid. That inner glow comes when you learn to contain that energy, returning it into the bloodstream, charging the blood with that prana. Sexual hormones are the essence of Kundalini. We tend to lose energy every day of our lives; women through their menstrual blood and men through their semen. We need to turn back this flow. With advanced techniques, all those hormones and nutrients in the menstrual flow can be returned to the system. See mention of the deer exercise in Sexual Kriya Activators, and find more documentation in Stephen Chang's *Tao of Sexology*.

There are several breathing techniques you can experiment with in Creative Masturbation and then later apply in lovemaking with your partner:

1) Focus on the energy in the genitals. Pull it up on the breath into the solar plexus or heart or third eye. The sexual energy will amplify and intensify whatever is going on at that chakra.

If you have trouble bringing the energy up to the heart or third eye, put a drop of saliva on that spot as a reference point. As the moisture evaporates, the cool sensation will help you to focus your consciousness. The energy will follow the consciousness and spread in a warm wave over the area as your heart or third eye opens. You will experience a tranquility which transcends the urgency of the raw sexual energy. This still is sexual energy, but it has been transmuted to a more subtle essence.

2) Pull the energy up chakra by chakra, as in Prana Mudra, Lesson 6.
3) Use the Hong-Sau Meditation, carrying the sexual energy on the natural rhythm of the breath. This relaxes the testicles and therefore delays ejaculation. If you are doing the technique properly, the breath will automatically stop and you will go into a Samadhi state, that awareness without the restriction of a physical body.

NOTE: Don't confuse Hong Sau Meditation (where the inhalation pulls Shiva energy from brow to base) with the breathing we practiced in Prana Mudra (where inhaling pulls Shakti energy up from the base).

4) Transmutation Breath I combines pranayam with bandha and mantra. That is especially effective to pull the energy into the brain.
5) Transmutation Breath II uses a different mantra. The effect is to diffuse the energy through the body.
6) Ultimately you will use the Cobra Initiation Breath which is far more powerful than any of these preliminaries.

NOTE: You can make the transmutation more intense by first balancing Ida and Pingala (Lesson 4).

Transmutation Breath 1:
To Concentrate Energy in the Brain

1) Inhale through the nose as you contract the anus.
2) With the breath pull sexual energy from the genitals up to the Third Eye.
3) Hold the breath for seven counts.
4) Take an extra sniff of air and project the breath from the Third Eye to the top of the head (Bindu).
5) Exhale through the nose as you mentally chant OM and relax the anus.
6) Chant OM only on the out-breath.
7) Do this breath/mantra seven times or until the sexual energy has been transmuted to the brain for rejuvenation.

The sensations produced by practicing this technique are:

- warmth all over the body,
- waves of vibrations in and around the body,
- tingling in the head, and
- expanding sensations in the head as you merge with the pulse of the Cosmic Orgasm.

Your head might feel overheated as the energy gathers. This means you are over-charging yourself. The energy should start diffusing over the body and feel like a cool, tranquil breeze. If you are feeling like the energy is congested, you have encountered a block. You should use Transmutation Breath 2 to relieve the congestion.

After you have transmuted the energy seven times, then you can have a normal orgasm and even ejaculate without a loss of energy. The essence has been retained.

Limit yourself to seven times. Eight is infinity, an abstract space. If you do the breath eight times you will go into a more abstract space than you can handle in the initial stages.

Transmutation Breath 2:
To Diffuse Energy Through the Body

1) Inhale through the nose as you contract the anus.
2) With the breath pull sexual energy from the genitals up to the Third Eye.
3) Think the mantra EE—AH—OH as you exhale and relax the anus. This mantra transmutes the energy in the semen and vaginal fluids, devitalizing the semen so it can be ejaculated without loss of energy.

SEXUAL POSITIONS

Shiva Dominant. In this position the man is able to alternate between thrusting and performing Aswini Mudra to build more intense energy.

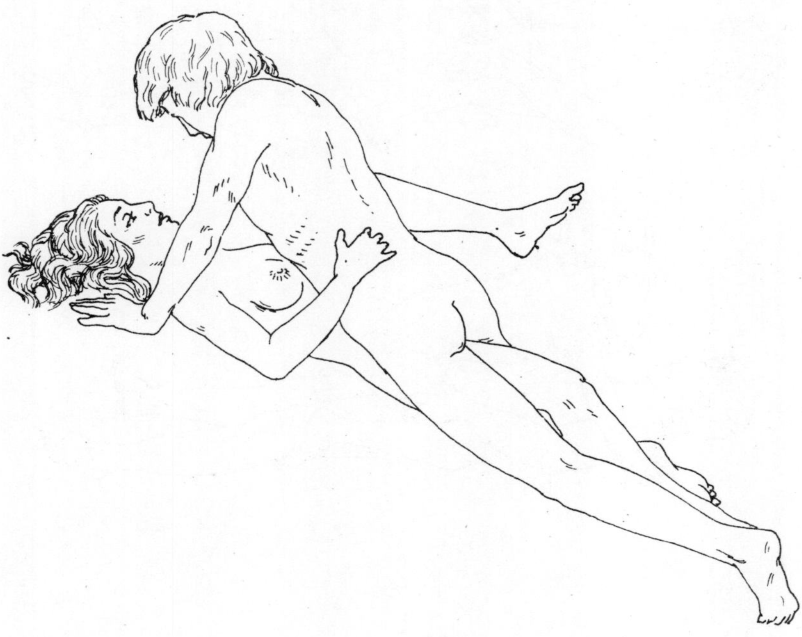

Shakti Dominant. In this position the male is totally passive. His partner is doing the Aswini Mudra contractions (a), and alternately thrusting her pelvis to receive maximum stimulation (b). She is actually milking the life force out of him into her to recirculate. When she has an orgasm, he begins to do Aswini Mudra and brings the vaginal secretions into the head of his penis to nourish him. This is not an abstraction. It actually happens.

Balanced Position. Here both are free to generate energy using the mudras and moving for stimulation.

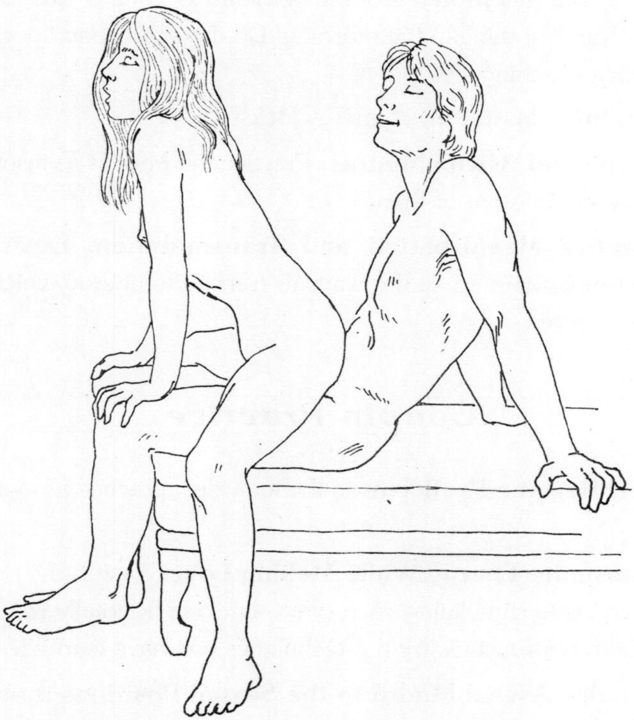

Individual Practice

1. Sexual Kriya Activators. Do as much as is necessary to get loosened up. Find some time each day to do a little "erotic dancing", with your own free-form use of the pelvic thrusts and circles. Do the Tummy Rub first thing in the morning. Do the squats and floor exercises while watching TV.

2. Bandhas. Master the 4 energy locks.

3. Vajroli and Aswini Mudras. Practice the Mudras as instructed until you feel mastery of them.

4. Creative Masturbation and Transmutation. Experiment with masturbation and all the ways to transmute energy which you have been given.

Couple Practice

1. First Become Proficient in the individual practice as indicated above.

2. Transmute Energy While Making Love. Take turns masturbating or orally stimulating each other. Let one be totally receptive. As orgasm approaches, try the techniques you have learned.

3. Practice Aswini Mudra in the Sexual Positions illustrated. The principle is the same as in masturbation. Use the Mudra to generate energy, along with any other stimulation you enjoy. At the orgasmic peak, transmute the energy.

Awareness

1. Stay Aroused. The true Tantrika maintains a constant state of arousal. All the time you are aroused, your sexual glands are secreting hormones and those are keeping you young and vital. You can keep yourself aroused all day by doing Aswini Mudra.

Before the course you may have felt that arousal demanded release, that feeling aroused meant you had to be hunting for a partner. You will have to let go of that idea.

Let it become a habit through the day to conserve the Apana energy with a Root Lock. Occasionally relax the sphincter muscle by pumping the energy. Learn to enjoy that slightly aroused state. If it becomes too intense, use one of the techniques for transmuting the energy. No one will know that you are stimulating yourself, but they will certainly notice that there is something fascinating about you a vibrancy, a charisma.

2. Notice How You Stop Your Energy. If you find your sexual energy toward your partner has diminished, you might look at the possibility that you are holding on to some grievances. Anger is the most powerful turn-off. Holding back sexual energy to punish a partner is another self-defeating game most of us play on occasion.

Notice what negativity toward your partner (or the opposite sex in general) comes into your inner monologue. Become conscious of this anger and its paralyzing effect on your sexuality.

Fear is the other block to sexual energy. All of us were programmed at a tender age, by well-intentioned parents and ministers, as to the dangers of sexual activity. As you stimulate the first two chakras all of your hidden fears will surface. Again, simply be aware of the fear, experience it as you Witness the experience, and let it go. Don't avoid the situations that bring up fear. Just jump in.

3. Be Aware of Risks. Avoiding pregnancy or sexually transmitted disease goes beyond our programmed fears. These are very practical concerns. Doing sexual acts in a spiritual context is not protection against these hazards. Use of a condom will not disturb the flow of energy. It actually provides another way to lengthen the lovemaking.

Lesson 10

Stimulation and Delay

Up to this point, the course has provided a background in the Yogic aspect of Tantric Kriya Yoga. Realize that the sexual part of Tantra is the lesser part. Letters we receive from prospective students reveal an expectation that Tantra will make them better lovers, more popular, more confident, more able to control their partners, and other motives very foreign to these studies. The last few lessons of this course are devoted to sexual material but in a spiritual context. The serious student is looking for a deeper experience of his Divine nature and using the sexual energy to propel him in that search. Those who are simply looking for bigger and better orgasms can find books and classes devoted just to that. When you have tired of that level of experience and want something deeper, then study Tantra.

Normal Sex has been charted by prominent sex researchers according to the rising and falling of intensity. It can be viewed in four stages. It begins with Excitement as you become aroused in foreplay, levels off into a Plateau, rises suddenly into a peak at Orgasm, and then falls off sharply in Resolution. For a man this can all happen very quickly - five to ten minutes start to finish.

A woman takes longer to become aroused, longer in plateau, her orgasm lasts longer and the resolution is not a plummeting line like a man's. She is ready to begin the process again much sooner and capable of several orgasms.

Many women don't achieve orgasm regularly, often because their mate doesn't take the time necessary to satisfy them. The distress that this causes has kept many therapists and magazines in

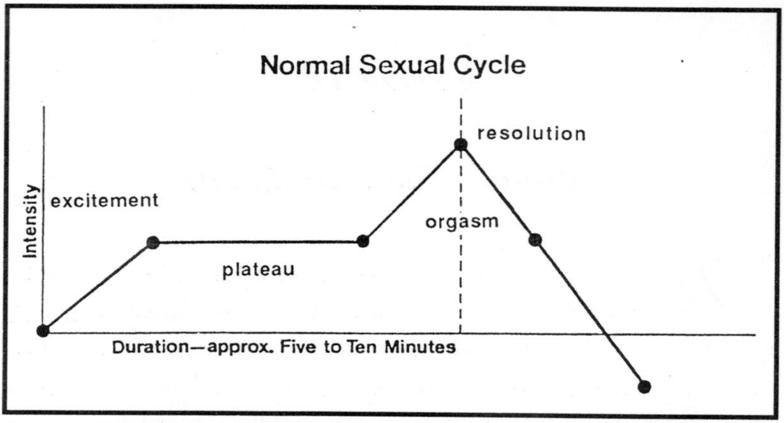

business for years as women keep looking for ways to experience greater satisfaction. As long as this culture was male dominated, very few women experienced sexual completion. Women have begun to demand their place in the last few years, so these matters have received a great deal of attention and research.

It is important to understand that the sexual experience is neurologically different for men than it is for women. The orgasm involves a different set of neurons at a different location in the brain. For the untrained man sex is a goal-oriented process. He feels a build-up of tension and an urgent need to release that tension as quickly as possible. It is a reflex response, rather like a knee jerking when you hit the right spot. Physiologically the process is identical to the behavior of lower mammals. Man is the slave of these tensions and they rule his life. This is why so many monastic orders have declared war on sexuality, figuring that total abstinence was the only way to deal with sexual tensions.

Orgasm is a problem for the man. He needs to feel like he is in control. He has a great ego investment in achieving orgasm. He worries about his "performance" and creates a lot of stress for himself, often impotence. He only gets one orgasm which might be an intense sensation, but not always. It is localized in the genitals and only lasts a moment. It leaves him exhausted, drained, ready for sleep.

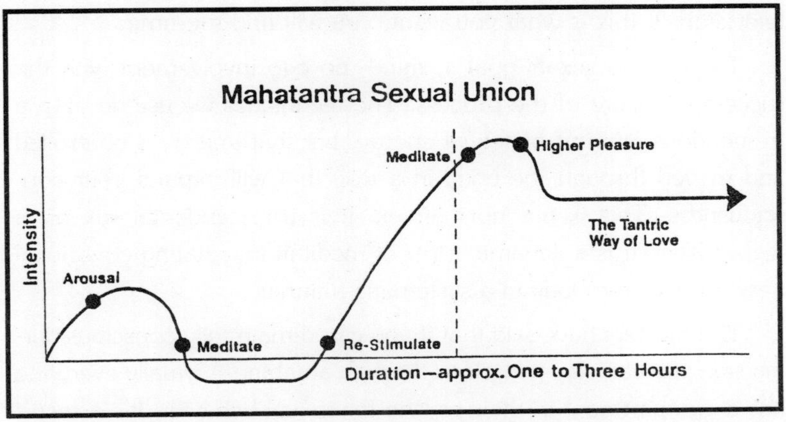

Tantric techniques were developed primarily for the man. He has always struggled with his sexuality, not knowing how to bring it into a spiritual context. He must learn to transcend his genetic endowment. The woman has the advantage. She already is tantric. Her orgasm occurs in an area of the brain that controls movement and touch. Her orgasms are deeper and longer, and can be repeated over and over. She is not so focused during sex and has the luxury of opening up into altered states of consciousness, out of body experiences, sense withdrawal, feeling mystical union with her partner, Samadhi. All of the goals the yogis spent lifetimes trying to achieve with their many techniques are available to a woman through sex; by nature of her physiology.

Rather than keep woman repressed, Tantra suggests that man learn from her. What she comes by naturally, he can attain with practice. He must learn to savor sexual energy, to delay its release, to surrender to it and let it propel him into higher states of consciousness.

Tantric Sex follows a very different pattern from "normal sex" and a different approach. The process is very slow and relaxed. You should set aside at least an hour, better yet two or three hours, uninterrupted. Most would protest they haven't that much time, and yet Americans spend an average of six hours a day watching television. If this is what you want, you will find the time.

There is no sexual goal in mind, no ego involvement with the success or failure of the process. The techniques we use develop a tremendous amount of sexual energy, but that energy is controlled and moved through the body in a way that will expand your consciousness. This is not normal sex. It is transcendental sex on a higher level. It is a dynamic form of meditation, rotating consciousness through the body in a systematic manner.

The masters have said that if you can remain fully conscious during sex, you can stay conscious through anything. Virtually everyone has a compartment in their psyche for sexual behavior. It's a secret act, something you are intensely embarrassed about if anyone "catches" you doing. We have been programed to be ashamed of our sexuality and in response had to create an alter ego, someone slightly apart from us, that is sexual. To reintegrate that exiled part back into your consciousness is a giant step forward.

The attitude of tantric lovers toward each other is one of worship. They look beyond the mundane concerns and ego positions. There is nothing to prove, no expectations to live up to. Each sees the other as the embodiment of the Universal Male or Female Principle. Each realizes that only by opening up to that Principle, by losing their identity in this union, can they find a place where there is neither male or female, just pure energy.

Arousal is different for man and woman. She pulls her Shakti energy up from the earth. Her first sense of arousal is a warmth spreading through her genitals and a desire to be close. It is that energy that triggers man's arousal. Shiva pulls his energy down from the heavens, drawn by the magnetism of Shakti. A man first experiences arousal in his brain with an image of his love goddess. That image then transfers to his genitals as he begins to feel aroused. With tantric practice, that energy will not be wasted. He will learn to pull it back up into his highest center so he can come into Samarasa, the enlightened state.

Excitement stage in Tantra is prolonged, allowing the woman ample time to activate her energy. The foreplay might go on for an hour before you reach that first orgasmic peak, an hour of gentle touching and soft kissing. You have learned in the Erotic Massage to stimulate each other's bodies in a systematic way so as to build a sensitivity so intense that every cell trembles with excitement. He must slowly open the petals of her lotus so that when he enters, when he reaches its heart, it will transform him into a precious jewel.

When the stimulation is working, you will see changes in your bodies that indicate arousal. Shakti will find her nipples have become hard and there is a wetness coming - that Dew of Immortality from her vagina. Shiva will have an erection. Both will feel muscular contractions in their genitals.

As excitement progresses the muscles around the anus will tighten, his penis will enlarge, as will her clitoris and vulva, turning red with engorgement of blood. Both Shiva and Shakti will feel a flush, as hormones trigger heat in their bodies. There might be a manifestation of Prana Shakti as heat and uncontrolled shaking.

A nourishment takes place during the excitement phase as sexual glands pour out hormones. The body is flooded with these elixers of youth, the true secret to rejuvenation. The longer the stimulation, the more hormones secreted.

Oral sex plays an important part in the tantric tradition. The mouth and tongue can provide a much more intense stimulation than the hands. Even intercourse doesn't provide as strong a sensation as oral congress. In more advanced Tantric training, these techniques are discussed in greater detail.

Orgasm. When the energy is approaching orgasm, you stop and transmute the energy. There are many techniques to delay orgasm, the most advanced being the Cobra Breath, which transmutes that intense energy and pulls it into the higher chakras. Western therapists would tell you to delay climax by thinking about the stock market or something unrelated. How hurtful it would be to pull away from your partner at this moment, when both of you are totally geared to coming together! Much better to focus entirely on the energy present, work with it, enjoy it.

When the energy level has subsided, you restimulate each other. Many stimulation techniques, particularly coupled with the energy locks, will maintain your arousal state indefinitely.

The next orgasmic peak will be higher than the first one as the energy has been allowed to build. At that very high peak, as you approach the point of no return, you once again delay and meditate. It takes some practice and a great deal of consciousness to be able to stop before the orgasm is out of your control. But each time you are able to delay and meditate, you go into a higher plateau. This tantric wave can extend for hours. You can tap into a higher pleasure state in the brain.

In that time the man can have several "internal orgasms" without ejaculation, without losing energy. The yogis claim that you must give up sexual activity in order to reach enlightenment because you lose energy with each ejaculation. The Tantric masters say that, if intercourse and climax are controlled, you will not lose energy, will not deplete your life force.

Semen is activated by a subtle energy called "ojas" (meaning strength or power). In the internal orgasm, a man draws that energy out of the sperm. His ejaculate is then devitalized, no longer capable of fertilizing an ovum, but his body is refreshed and energized.

Woman releases an "ejaculate" in orgasm, which contains an energy-rich hormone that her partner can absorb through his penis, or he can ingest if she climaxes while he is stimulating her orally. This hormone is of great importance to the man. It is his role to stimulate her enough to bring her to that orgasmic point.

Prolonged sex takes strength and stamina. You must be in good physical condition to maintain this arousal. It also takes control on his part to keep delaying his climax. This comes through breath control and dedication to the long range results of tantric practice.

When woman reaches her climax she totally surrenders herself and feels the Kundalini energy explode through her entire body. It rushes up her spine, opening the chakras as it passes. This lasts about six seconds for a woman unschooled in tantric practice. But using the transmutation processes, she can keep that explosion going as long as she wishes. It's much like a surfer catching the wave and riding it out rather than getting caught and swamped by it.

Through mastery of Tantra both man and woman can have many climaxes much more intense than they ever dreamed possible, charging the whole nervous system, thrilling their entire body. For that moment their ego will be dissolved and they will feel at one with the Ultimate Universal Unity.

Resolution. When you have finished, your nervous system will feel totally relaxed, and you will feel the rejuvenation that has occurred. You will be open to ESP and healing energies. You will be able to project love and gratitude to your partner.

During orgasm, polarities switch. A woman becomes more male, more verbal, wanting to communicate. A man feels his female energy most at that time. He may be uncomfortable in that unfamiliar energy and want to escape from it. The man must be willing to allow his female part to be expressed.

Immediately after orgasm we are in a most vulnerable state, hyper-suggestible. Any comment made at this time can have far-reaching effects. Criticism at this moment can be devastating. Expressions of love can be transforming. Hopefully at this time you can just lie together, holding each other, just being close, projecting love to each other non-verbally. This after-glow can be as important as the act of love itself. It puts you into a psychic attunement with each other.

Many men fear vulnerability and aren't willing to stay present in that situation. He grabs a cigarette to stifle the energy, and then quickly escapes in sleep, leaving her feeling used, abandoned, and angry. This time is precious for solidifying the relationship. Very few people are sexually satisfied. Most have a deep sense that something is missing. Communion and a deep intimacy is what they really need, but they must have the courage to be available for it to happen.

STIMULATION

Initial arousal is stimulated in three ways: 1) Fantasy or imaging of past or future sexual experiences; 2) Sensory experiences of what you see, hear, smell and taste; and 3) Direct physical stimulation by touch.

Imaging is fantasy carried to a luxurious extreme. Remember, the central nervous system can't distinguish between real experience and intensely imagined experience, and it doesn't care where its stimulation comes from. To image is especially valuable for women to prepare their bodies for sexual encounter, to get a head start so there is not such a gap between their arousal period and their mate's. This is also a way to generate stronger and more lasting orgasm. Men usually fantasize without any prompting.

Remember a previous sexual experience which was particularly satisfying. Recreate in your mind what was happening in all the senses. Hear the music in the background and the sound of his voice; smell the incense that was burning or the fireplace aroma; and the scent your beloved was wearing; taste the wine you sipped together and the taste of his body as you licked and sucked its every part, see the image of his body silhouetted by the candlelight, feel the touch of his fingers running through your hair, of his lips at your breast, and finally of his lingam filling you, exploding inside you, pulling you into rapture.

Then take that memory and expand upon it. Add all the details that might have happened, that you wished had happened. See him stimulating you in all the ways you ever imagined. See yourself in sexual positions you never tried before, in places and situations you would never dare to try. Watch yourself experiencing orgasm after orgasm. You are limited only by your power to visualize. Once again it is true that what you can visualize you can manifest. The clearer your image of it is, the more vibrant and lifelike the image, the more able you are to bring it into reality.

It is best to do your imaging <u>in anticipation</u> of a rendezvous with your lover. While the imagination is a powerful tool and good preparation, it is still dealing with past memories and anticipated future pleasures. The goal of any meditation is to bring you into the present.

Sensory Experiences in the moment bring you closer to the state of meditation. Many spiritual paths teach denial of the senses. Tantra seeks to explore every sensation, taking each to its most exquisite level, not becoming attached to the sensation, but making of it a meditation, focusing on the sensation in the moment WITH TOTAL AWARENESS as if nothing else existed. This focus brings you into the eternal now, the only true meditation. As long as some unexplored curiosity is clinging in your mind, the thoughts will continue to jump around. Only when you have fully explored the world of sensation are you ready to drop it, and then experience the stillness of meditation.

Remember each chakra is associated with a sense, with one of the 12 cranial nerves that surround the pineal gland. To stimulate a sense is to stimulate a chakra.

Through the sense of SIGHT comes most of our awareness of the world. It is very important to prepare a place for making love that is warm, interesting, conducive to sexual energy. Select vivid colors. Reds are particularly stimulating, while blue takes you into an abstract space. Always make love in the light, subdued light perhaps, but never in darkness. If you find yourself uncomfortable or self-conscious in the light, that is a sure sign that you have partitioned off your sexual nature and only allow it to function in anonymity. For you, it is essential to stay with the discomfort or embarrassment, in the same objective, detached way you have learned to watch all your quirks as they come to the surface of consciousness.

The sense of SMELL is deeply rooted in our primal nature. It's related to the first chakra, the vestigial remains of our animal nature. It is a powerful impetus for sexual energy. Scents that resemble sexual secretions are the most powerful triggers. Some interesting research was done with monkeys. The sexual organs were surgically removed from several females so there was no trace of hormonal secretions. Placed in a cage with males these animals were ignored. Then secretions from the sexual organs of healthy females were rubbed onto the test females. The males went into a frenzy, vying for their attention and the pleasure of their company. Don't discount your animal nature. It's part of you. Honor it and use it to your advantage.

Since first chakra energy is stimulus-response oriented, it is very much subject to conditioning. A certain fragrance of incense burning during a wonderful meditation can condition you so that the next time you smell that incense you will go deeply into meditation. It's important to create the same environment to take advantage of this fact of your nature. If you are a smoker, you probably haven't smelled anything for years and are at a distinct disadvantage here.

Your sense of TASTE is related to the second chakra. Taste is dependent upon smell, just as second chakra is dependent upon first. If you are accustomed to watching TV or reading or talking while you eat, you probably haven't tasted anything for a long time. Living consciously includes every activity of your life. Let the food you share with your beloved be tasted with total awareness. As you taste each other let your attention be totally there.

Your sense of HEARING can pull you into wonderful spaces. We've spoken already of the powers of mantra. Many other sounds can evoke a variety of moods. You might find that listening to primitive drums will arouse an energy that doesn't usually come to surface.

Certain music can play on your heart and open up your emotional center. Some sublime music can carry you off into the cosmos.

Men are usually more visual in their orientation and women more aural. When you attune yourself to the medium that is not your usual experience, it can flip you into uncharted spaces. We have seen engineers - totally left-brained male energy, fascinated by classical music because only under its influence could they open up to their female aspect. The music was their key to meditation.

Physical Stimulation takes advantage of your sense of TOUCH, and from that comes the most exquisite experiences possible. If you don't particularly enjoy being touched, it may be a hold-over from infancy when you desperately longed for touching and didn't get it. Institutionalized infants, given adequate food and diapering, but deprived of touch, sometimes wither and die. It is essential to human survival. You need it, and you want it.

If you're denying that need, it's probably to protect yourself from remembering that primal pain. If you are doing the exercises in this course, this is all going to come to the surface. You must relive, and be the Witness to, this painful memory so that it can release and leave you free to receive pleasure from touch.

We could easily devote an entire book to the many ways partners can stimulate and pleasure each other, and the resistance people have to intimacy and to giving and receiving pleasure. Not too surprisingly, there are many such books available for those who wish to explore further.

What we can add to that vast body of arousal techniques is the metaphysical aspect, to help you understand what's happening in the energy bodies. You are learning the alchemy of transmuting that energy, once aroused, for use in advancement of the spirit and rejuvenation of the body.

To review the points already made about stimulation:

1) Take plenty of time. Allow for at least one-half hour of stimulation and one-half hour of intercourse
2) Arouse the entire body before touching primary zones (see Erotic Massage).
3) Maintain a balance between giving and receiving stimulation, even if you would rather do one or the other. Stimulating each other simultaneously has an advantage over taking turns in that both of you stay aroused and can pull each other to greater heights to balance your arousal states. When Shakti is aroused, Shiva is automatically triggered by the magnetism of her energies.
4) Focus on primary erogenous zones (lips, breasts, genitals) when building toward climax. Then move to secondary erogenous zones and do delay or transmuting techniques to diffuse the energy through the body until the entire body is brought to a peak.

Lips and Tongues

There is a subtle nerve circuit running from the lips through the hard palate, down the front of the body to the genitals. Another channel runs up the spine. There is a "switch" point in the hard palate that completes the circuit.

Using that front channel, a woman s upper lip is directly connected to her clitoris and a man's lower lip is directly linked to his penis: If they kiss so that she sucks and nibbles his lower lip as he sucks and nibbles her upper lip, they will arouse great sexual energy, particularly if they are doing Vajroli Mudra and breathing deeply. Of course, any other form of kissing is also stimulating.

Either one can complete that circuit by touching their own tongue to the roof of their mouth (as in Khechari Mudra). Touching the area just behind the teeth directly stimulates the penis as well as the pituitary gland. Pulling the tongue top as far back as possible stimulates the Yoni as well as the pineal gland. Even more powerful is one tongue touching the palate of the other so that their circuits are merged. A woman can greatly arouse her man by "giving him her tongue." Her tongue tip touches the pressure point just behind his teeth, that completes a circuit for him and energy rushes to his penis.

Breasts

Sucking a woman's breast is, for many women, enough stimulation to bring her to orgasm. The nipples are connected to the Ida-Pingala caduceus. Those two channels cross at the sexual chakra, so the connection is quite direct and very strong. For a man to lie quietly and suck, like an infant nursing, for a prolonged period - ten to twenty minutes - is a marvelous gift to his mate and to himself.

A woman can transmute the arousal she experiences, inhaling that excitement up her spine to the heart. She can exhale, giving the energy through her nipples, to her lover. He receives from her a profound nurturing, a nourishment, of Divine Mother's milk. This is a skill a Tantric woman must develop.

The entire breast needs to be stroked, not just the nipples, although that is the most sensitive part. The breast is designed to feed an infant, and the baby's hands often hold the breast. Nature has designed the female body so the nursing process is intensely pleasurable for the mother, just to make sure the infant receives what it needs.

A man might be uncomfortable with his partner's breasts. If his infant experiences with nursing were disturbing, this "nursing" might bring it to the surface. If his mother resented or refused to nurse him, or he was bottle fed by someone who wasn't bonded to him, that deep soul nourishment that comes from nursing was denied him. That could still be very painful. If reluctance to "nurse" comes up, be the Witness of it. To avoid that pain by avoiding your partner's breasts is cheating both of you of the richest lovemaking experiences.

Every woman I have ever known who has developed breast cancer has had a long relationship with a man (or series of men) who had a closed heart, who would not receive the energy that needs to flow through the breasts.

Many men have never developed sensitivity in their nipples. As you allow your female energy to manifest, you will find your nipples give you more pleasure. If your heart is closely guarded, breast stimulation might be irritating. As your heart opens, stimulation becomes most pleasurable. A woman can give as much attention to her partner's breasts as he gives to hers.

Genitals

There are many books, even videos, describing every possible way to stroke and suck the genitals. You need a working knowledge of genital anatomy and stimulation. Many people are embarrassed about "private parts" and have no conscious awareness of their body or their lover's.

Physically and metaphysically there are correspondences between male and female genitalia.

MALE SEXUAL ANATOMY

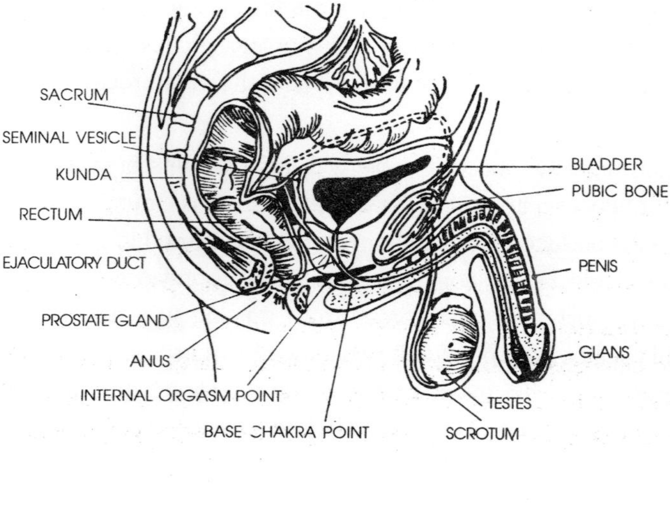

The clitoris is a female penis and responds similarly. Both clitoris and penis become erect during arousal, both enjoy being stroked, licked and sucked, and both become very sensitive just before and after orgasm, so much so that they would often rather not be touched in that interval. The clitoral orgasm resembles the normal male orgasm in that it is brief, localized, and doesn't lead to rapture. Interesting to note, the clitoris is the only organ that has no function besides pleasure. It has the same number of nerve endings as a penis, and so is a highly condensed, extremely sensitive organ.

The male prostate gland has as its female counterpart the G-Spot, which in Tantra is referred to as the Sacred Spot. The actual root chakra in the female body is located high in the vagina, on the back wall, near the cervix. Stimulating that point directly is dangerous because the cervix is easily irritated. Stimulating the Sacred Spot serves to excite the female root energies.

Both prostate and Sacred Spot develop out of the same embryonic tissue. Both find pressure unpleasant before arousal. It produces an urge to urinate. When the body is approaching orgasm, both respond to touch with exquisite sensations that prolong and

FEMALE SEXUAL ANATOMY

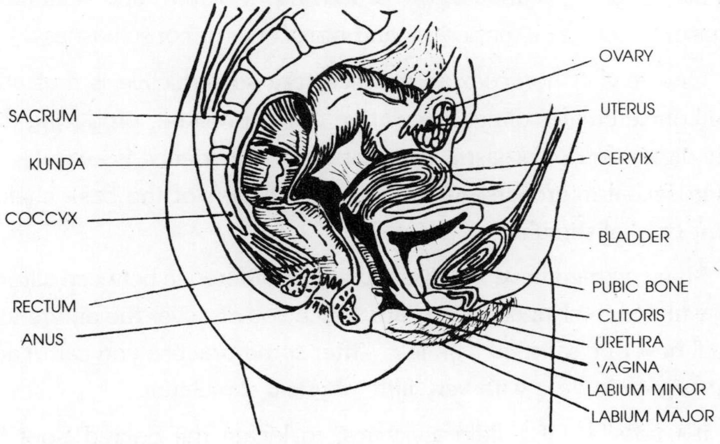

intensify the orgasm. At climax, both release copious fluids with similar chemical composition. For the male this fluid is the vehicle for transporting semen. For the female it is a delicious nectar, prized by the erotic connoisseur. It has only recently come to light that woman produces ejaculate, contrary to common belief.

There is a small gland just beneath the sacrum, referred to in ancient texts as the Kunda gland, where Kundalini is said to reside. Stimulation of the root chakra serves to activate the dormant energies of the Kunda gland.

The spot we have designated as the Base Chakra, on the perineum, is the closest external point to the prostate gland on a man. A woman's Sacred Spot is accessed directly through her vagina.

Stroking that point on your aroused partner has three effects. 1) It produces very pleasurable sensations, 2) It delays climax so the energy can build up to a higher level, (assuming your partner is doing Aswini Mudra) and 3) when you release the point and your partner takes the Transmutation Breath, the energy explodes and propels Kundalini up the spine. This point can be used for stimulation, delay, and transmutation.

When a man's orgasm develops in this way, it is the same as a female orgasm, capable of producing multiple and extended orgasms, mystical experiences and transcendent consciousness.

One reason homosexual practices are so seductive is that anal intercourse creates direct stimulation of the prostate, producing this new dimension of orgasm. But that same experience is available in heterosexual intercourse by manual stimulation of the base chakra point or anal stimulation.

Many women have not discovered the difference between clitoral orgasm and the Kundalini orgasm. Once you discover the difference, you'll never be satisfied with less. After some practice you can reach that orgasmic state with very little physical stimulation.

It's possible, if a little awkward, to locate the Sacred Spot by yourself. You or your partner can insert a finger into the vagina and explore the front wall in the area 1 to 3 inches up,.looking for a rough tissue. There's some variation in its location. Only look for it when aroused, or the sensations will not be particularly pleasant.

Once you have discovered the Sacred Spot, you can experiment with different sexual positions that allow stimulation of that point. You must find what works for you, considering the wide variation in angle of erection, size and shape of genitals, etc. Use other positions, or manual or oral stimulation, to get the clitoris aroused, then move into a position to connect with the Spot. The following three positions work well.

She is entirely in control of the angle of penetration and can stimulate first her clitoris, then her Sacred Spot.

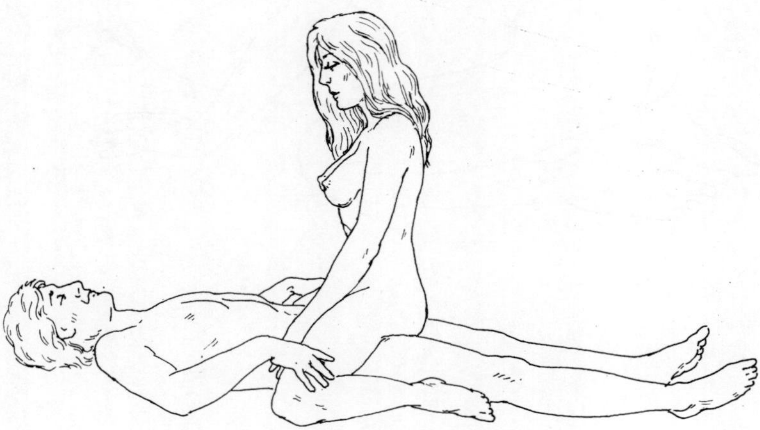

She can adjust the angleof penetration to stimulate the Sacred Spot. A pillow under her hips might help.

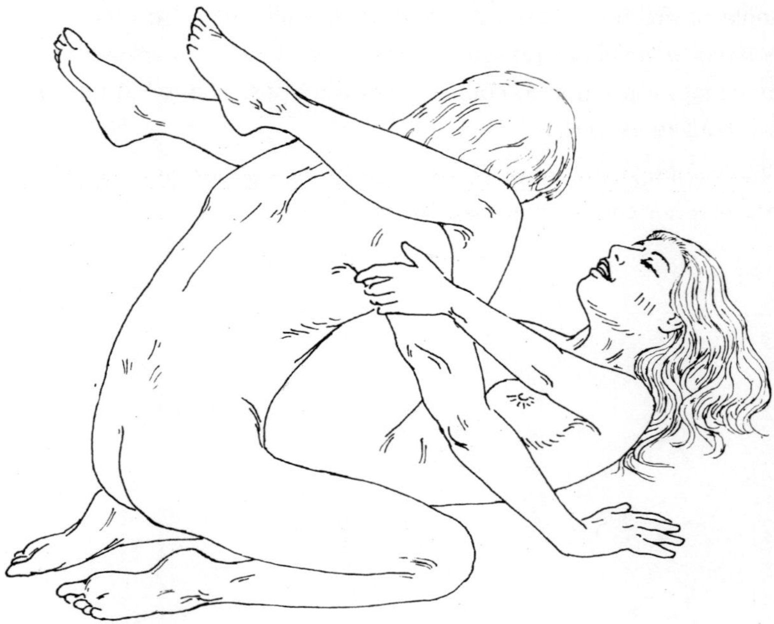

He can alternate between shallow thrusts (to stimulate her clitoris) and deep thrusts to reach the Sacred Spot.

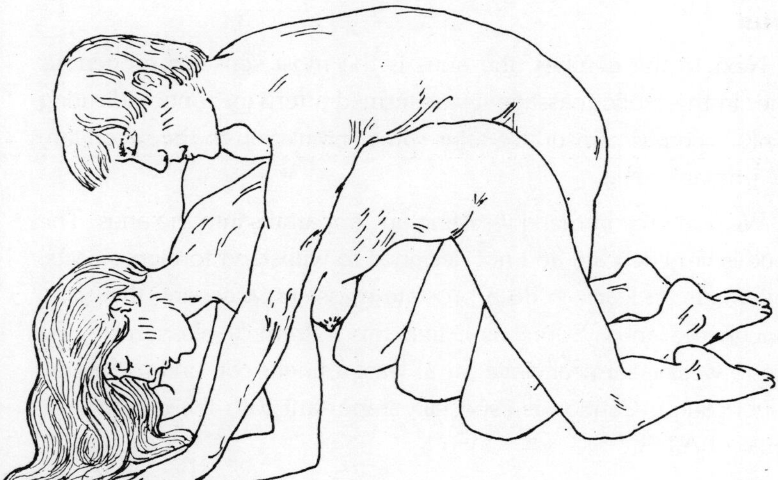

Testicles

A gentle circular squeezing of the testicles stimulates them to deliver more sperm (whose energy you can recycle). The touching feels wonderful to the man, and the extra energy produces a more intense orgasm. His partner can perform this stimulation manually or orally. This is a very vulnerable place in the male body and must be treated with the greatest sensitivity.

Anus

Next to the genitals, the anus is the most sensitive erogenous zone. In the erotic massage it was termed a tertiary zone, indicating it only becomes pleasurable after some stimulation to the secondary and primary zones.

We don't recommend inserting any apparatus into the anus. The tissue is very delicate and not designed to withstand foreign objects. A woman can learn to do a prostate massage, accessing the gland through the anus. Some men find this extremely pleasurable. Be sure to wear a surgical glove, or at least a finger cot, and use plenty of lubrication. Caution is especially important with the current epidemic of AIDS.

For external stimulation, use the pad of your middle finger to massage the anus. Stroke around the anus, and press and release as your partner does Aswini Mudra. Your "massage" serve both to stimulate and to assist your partner in containing the energy. You can do this at any point in the lovemaking. However if a man has touched the woman's anus, that same hand should not touch the vagina, for obvious hygienic reasons.

Total Body

Don't get so engrossed in genitalia that you forget the rest of the body. Continue to involve lips, breasts, and secondary zones.

DELAY TECHNIQUES

As Orgasm Approaches, You Can Choose to 1) Delay, 2) Transmute, or 3) Surrender. You might want to delay climax several times to build up a greater charge of energy. When you finally feel the energy is as intense as you can manage, you are ready to transmute. Sometimes it will feel right to just go with the orgasm and not attempt any technique.

You should try to get seven Cobra Breaths (or Transmutation Breaths) before surrendering to the orgasm. Even then, continue to stimulate the Sacred Spot so orgasm will be longer and more intense.

Delay Techniques for Women

1. Relax any tension that might be present in the body. (Tension-Relaxation - Lesson 1).
2. Breathe very deeply and slowly to diffuse the energy buildup. (Complete Breath - Lesson 2).
3. Practice Hong Sau meditation. (Lesson 8).
4. Stop the direct stimulation until the energy subsides a bit. Have some signal so your partner knows to move to a less sensitive area.
5. Stop doing Vajroli or Aswini Mudras. (Lesson 9) You should be contracting and relaxing most of the time, except when delaying or transmuting.
6. Apply a Root Lock and hold. When you let go, the energy will shoot up your spine.

Delay Techniques for Men

Any of the techniques given for women can be used early in arousal by men, but they may not be strong enough to stop a male orgasm that's ready to peak.

1. **Eye Rolling.** All energy moves clockwise. When you reverse that by moving counter-clockwise, you disperse the energy.
   a) Take a deep breath and hold for 16 counts.
   b) Do Khechari Mudra.
   c) Roll the eyes counter-clockwise three times.
   d) Tense the anus muscle.
   e) Exhale and relax the anus muscle.
   f) Repeat three times, then continue sexual union. Once you have control, resume anal contractions.

Using this technique, a man can continue in sexual intercourse two or three hours or more. A woman could use this technique, but it's a little more extreme than she would normally need. Be sure your partner knows what you are doing. It might be a little unnerving for a new partner to see you performing this technique.

2. **Tantric Locking of the Base Chakra**

To Delay.
   a) Take three deep slow breaths.
   b) Breathing naturally, use the index and middle finger to apply pressure on the Base chakra point. (perineum) If your partner is in the right position, she could do it for you.
   c) Releasing the pressure, take a deep breath and do Khechari Mudra until you have control.

To Extend Orgasm. Alternately press and release the base chakra point.

To Produce a Kundalini Rush. Maintain pressure on the base chakra and hold the Root Lock. Release both simultaneous with the orgasmic peak as you take the Cobra (or Transmutation) Breath.

3. Testicle Pull

To Delay. As a man approaches orgasm, the scrotal sac pulls up tight against the body. Gently grasp the scrotum and pull it away from the body to delay climax.

To Transmute. You can do the Testicle Pull while transmuting energy with the breath and mantra.

For Internal Orgasm. You can use the Testicle Pull to intensify an Internal Orgasm. Press the point at the base of the penis while pulling the testicles.

To Surrender. If you chose to have a regular orgasm, you can prolong it by alternately pulling and releasing the scrotum. We encourage methods that conserve the energy, but you always have a choice of "getting off."

In any of the above processes, the woman can manipulate the testicles, with her partner's guidance.

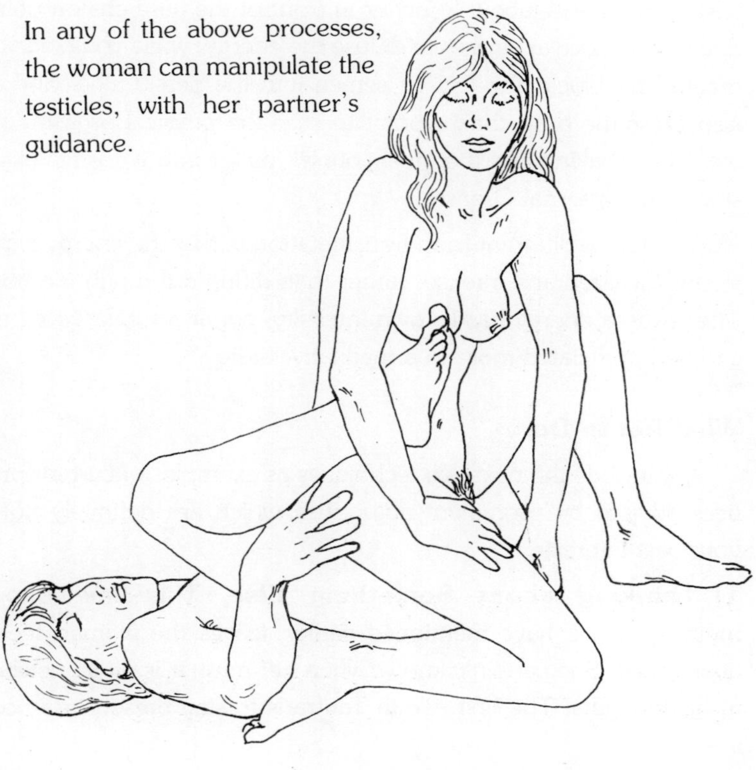

Internal Orgasm.

In Mahatantra, the great Tantra, you go beyond physical orgasm to internal orgasm where you don't have an outer ejaculation. These feel much like a regular orgasm, localized at the genitals, but are more intense, more pleasurable, involve the whole body. Since no semen is lost, you can maintain an erection and have several such orgasms. The life-essence of the semen, plus its nutritive value, are reabsorbed by the etheric and physical bodies, respectively.

Your partner can stroke your penis with one hand, and gently squeeze your testicles with her other hand. This stimulates the testicles to produce more sperm. The penile stimulation pulls in solar energy to vitalize the sperm.

When you are at the brink of climax, she will press a point at the base of the penis (about 2 inches in front of the base chakra point). She rubs in circular strokes to diffuse the energy, while you hold your breath.This blocks the flow of semen into the penile tube. She will also press the base chakra point to stop the physical orgasm. You may start shaking and then feel yourself pulled into a cosmic explosion of the Internal Orgasm.

NOTE: This is different from transmutation in that the energy explosion is localized and intense, rather than diffused through the body. The diffused energy has its own intensity, but at a subtler level, and can be appreciated more in a meditative state.

What Not to Do.

We include the next two techniques as examples of current practices advised by prominent authorities which are <u>definitely</u> <u>not</u> in your best interests.

1) Thinking about Something Else. This time-honored method, as we have mentioned earlier, leaves the woman feeling abandoned. She certainly knows when her partner is off somewhere in his thoughts. The first rule in Tantra is to stay present, stay conscious! This is an unacceptable technique.

2) The Squeeze Technique. When orgasm is imminent, a man squeezes the tip of his penis to delay the climax. If he is trying to prolong orgasm, he alternately squeezes and relaxes. This well-known practice is uncomfortable, ineffective, and potentially dangerous. This allows the semen to enter the urethra. If for some reason he doesn't ejaculate, that semen will drain back into the bladder where it can bring on bladder infection or prostatitis. Once the semen is in the penis it must be released. The point of using the techniques we recommend is to keep it from getting that far.

A SCENARIO

They had lost themselves in exploring each other's bodies, in touching and tasting. He had approached her so slowly, nibbling her ears, her neck, but reverently bypassing her breasts, stroking her inner thighs, but just brushing her genitals. After a while the bypassed parts called out, begging to be touched, and so he did.

It seemed as though they could know each others' minds, so attuned they had become. What started as a lustful attraction had transcended to a communion. He had been drawn by her beauty, but now he was seeing a deeper beauty that moved him to a state of worship. She could sense the transformation, and knew that he was aware of the Goddess within her. And so there was no further need to hide that energy. She felt her connection with the earth grow stronger, and tapped into its life-force as her anal muscles pulsed in contraction. The lips of her vagina parted, flushed and swollen as the earth filled her womb with life giving energy. She felt a tingling in her Venus Mound. Unable to wait another moment, he entered her.

The power of her arousal was awe inspiring. As he gazed at this incredible being he felt light-headed and a rush of energy filled his penis. He thought it would explode, but it was much too soon. This moment must be prolonged. He had been rhythmically contracting his anus, and the energy had built to unmanageable levels. He knew what to do. Pulling his tongue back into his mouth and breathing deeply, he rolled his eyes several times to disperse the intensity of the energy. Now he is ready to go on.

Moments later she is feeling a mounting intensity that will soon crest into an orgasmic wave. She offers her tongue to his willing mouth and he again feels a surge of energy rush into his genitals. They move so slowly, with such grace.

When she begins to climax, she breathes a deep breath again and again that pulls that orgasmic wave throughout her body. Her anal muscles and vagina are contracting, which produces fantastic feelings for him. Once again he needs to exercise control. It just takes a few seconds to touch the safeguard point. It was a higher peak this time.

There is little movement in her climax, no flailing and moaning. Most of the movement is her internal contractions. She pulls him closer and her energy begins shooting through him. He scarcely moves, not wanting to miss any of the subtle feast she has offered him.

She is sucking his lower lip and he her upper lip as their energy bodies merge. She has finished with the meditation and surrenders herself to the rush of orgasmic energy, so intense and yet so relaxed. As she opens herself up more and more the dimensions of the energy expand and he is pulled along into this great void where nothing is and everything is.

He is aware that she is touching a point under his penis, and though he has just had an intense orgasm, his erection is still strong and he is filled with energy.

Now she rests for a moment, but is by no means finished. He lays back as she mounts him. He moves slowly and gently, just enough to keep his erection, thrusting deeper into her vagina, producing more pressure on her clitoris. She starts moving up and down with some experimentation to find the angle that will give her the

the most stimulation, first to the clitoris and then to the magic Sacred Spot. They both continue to do the anal contractions. He feels her rhythmic squeezes massaging his throbbing member. This dynamic interplay is sucking him into another dimension.

He can bear it no more. He stops moving, and she does too. He breathes deeply and feels the energy suffuse through his body with the breath. He begins to mentally chant OM OM OM. A ringing fills his head to match the intensity of the imminent explosion in his genitals. And then these two concentrations of energy become one as his body is filled with wave after wave of light.

When it has subsided, he looks at this Goddess who has transported him to such uncharted dimensions. Her energy was the booster that propelled him out into the Void, where he felt so profoundly at home. Amazed and grateful to be part of something so much bigger than life, they hold each other and feel that this moment will never end.

Individual Practice

While this lesson has considered techniques for couples, all of these practices can be included in your Auto-Erotic Meditation. In fact, it is easier to achieve mastery by yourself, without a partner. Practice stimulating yourself and delaying and extending the orgasm. Practice transmuting in all the ways that have been presented.

Couple Practice

This entire lesson is a couple practice.

Awareness

1. Look Back at Your Sexual History Write in some detail the patterns you have established when you want sex - the settings, the partners, the positions, the time allowed. It is important to bring into consciousness what has been going on as a habit. To write it down you must bring it into very clear focus. Right now it is probably quite hazy, since our sexual natures have been forced to carry on their activities slightly removed from consciousness.

2. Write Your Own Version of a Scenario. Pretend you are writing for an erotic magazine, determined to present a tantric session, instead of the hackneyed stuff one typically finds in such magazines. If you come up with something especially nice, please send it to us and we will print it in our Tantric Journal!

The point is not to be a great writer. It is to make yourself visualize very clearly how tantric love works. If you can't see it in your mind, you probably can t do it. Anything you can visualize, you can manifest.

Lesson 11

Positions and Circuits

Inidividual Solar-Lunar Circuit.

In each human body is a potential circuit to balance the solar and lunar energies. Without training, that circuit is not often completed and the energy remains out of balance (i.e. excessively solar or lunar).

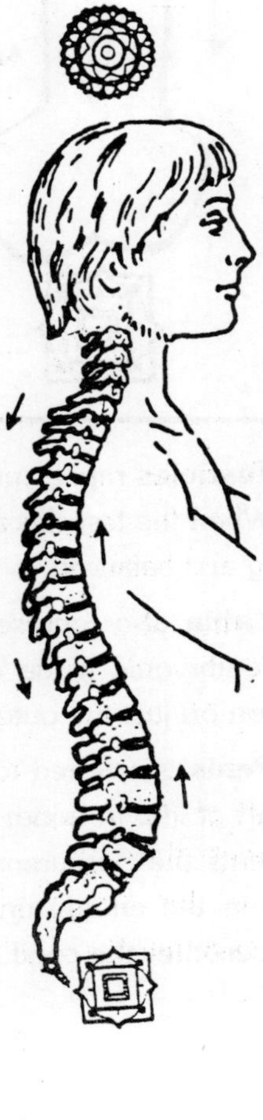

We have looked at solar energy in Pingala, the channel on the right side of the spine. It is also true that solar energy runs down the back of the spine.

We have seen lunar energy in Ida, the subtle channel on the left side of the spine. It's also true that lunar energy flows up the front of the spine.

Actually, the two currents form a double helix around the spine, which can be viewed from either front or side perspective. Either model is useful for these techniques.

The raised tongue in Khechari Mudra is a switch to complete this circuit, provided the body/mind is pure enough to carry the energy. Rotating the energy through this circuit is the essence of Tantric Kriya Yoga and other advanced spiritual trainings.

Genital Solar-Lunar Circuits.

The energy circuits in the genitals represent symbolically and functionally the currents of the entire body.

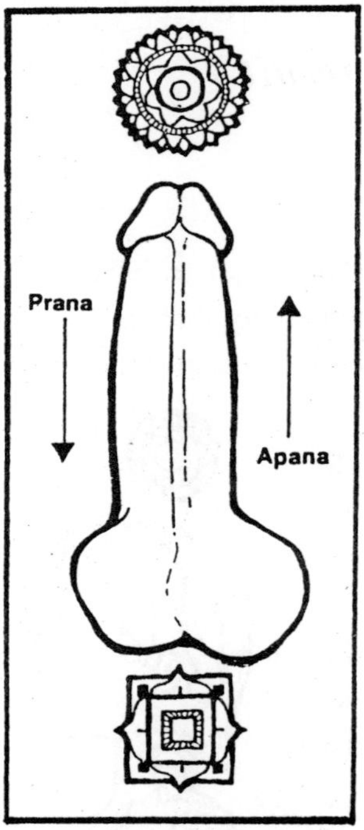

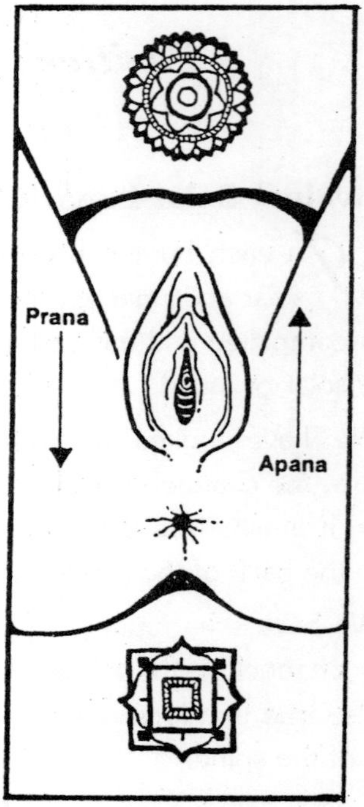

The Testicles represent Ida and Pingala, the lunar and solar channels. When the testicles are properly stimulated, Ida and Pingala are flowing and balanced.

The Labia also represent Ida and Pingala. They derive from the same embryonic tissue as the scrotum. Stroking in the indicated direction on just the outer labia brings that energy balance.

The Penis is referred to in classical texts as the Muradanda Staff, the staff of life, in honor of the life-generating force it expresses. It represents the Sushumna canal. A man applies the root lock and builds up the energy under pressure, so when he ejaculates, the penis becomes the conduit for a rush of Kundalini energy.

In much the same way, with pressure built up, Kundalini could rush up his spine. Ejaculation is to man a preview of what the Kundalini experience offers, as the sensations are very similar. And of course it's also a trap. For sensations so pleasurable, man is willing to pay the enormous cost in energy. Orgasm drains his reserve of Kundalini force and denies him the possibility of that experience. Without Tantra a man would have to make the difficult choice to give up the immediate pleasure of orgasm and work toward the Kundalini experience. With Tantra such choice is not necessary. He can conserve his energy and still have the pleasure of orgasm.

There are five kinds of pranic energy, one for each element. The earth energy, Apana, is controlled by the first chakra. There the earth energy enters and leaves the body. The tip of the penis is an entry point for solar energy, as is the crown of the head. Sitting in the sunlight you can pull in solar energy through the tip of the penis with visualization and the breath, and direct it to the testicles where it electrifies the sperm.

As the energy begins to move in the penis, it will feel hot at the tip (sun) and cool at the base (earth). Performing the Root Lock to keep Apana from escaping creates pressure. As you masturbate and do the breathing technique you can feel the energy cycling back and forth along the cord of the penis between the poles. This is your Kundalini life-circuit.

The Clitoris serves the same function as the penis, with its tip as the solar head. Again the first chakra serves as the entry point for earth energy. The point on the perineum, equivalent to a man's first chakra point, is the closest external point to woman's first chakra, but as we have discovered, the real point lies several inches inside, and can be reached directly through the vagina. That is why a woman doing the Root Lock must involve the vaginal muscles as well as the anal.

Couple Solar-Lunar Circuit.

When a couple comes into union consciously, they move their energy simultaneously. Their cooperative efforts are far more rewarding than individual effort. Two minds joined in a single thought create a powerful force. Their strength and weakness balance each other. She can easily pull magnetic energy in at the base. That magnetism draws his electrical energy down from his head. Balancing the male-female aspects allows them to move the energy back up.

We are each encased in an auric egg, an energy field with positive and negative poles. When you connect with a partner you set up a complete energy circle in the couple as it is with the cosmos. Once that circuit is connected it will vibrate, each chakra in resonance with its own frequency.

Different positions create different energy movements. In many tantric texts and much erotic art there are sexual positions which most Westerners could not possibly get into. As we have said, Indians are accustomed to squatting and so the lotus position comes easily to them. A lifetime of sitting on chairs has made these positions impossible for us. But don't be discouraged.

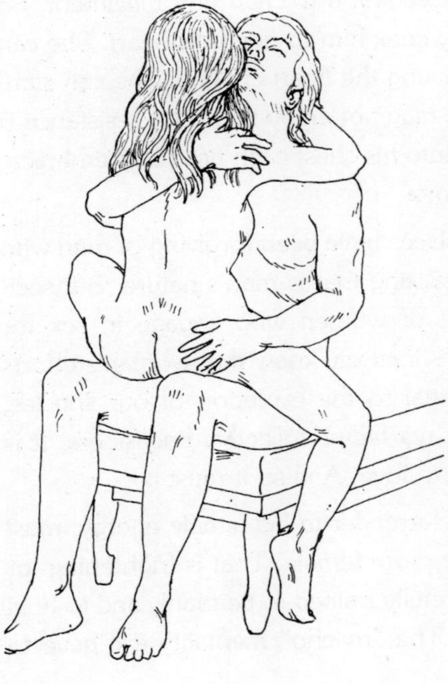

If you are not comfortable in the classical Yab-Yum position (pg. 198 these two variations are equally effective.

In tantric love the only consideration is that the spine must be relatively straight. Then when you take the Cobra Breath up, the spinal energy can travel unimpeded. You will learn to create a cosmic circuit between you and your mate.

The Heart-Genital Circuit.

Besides the solar-lunar polarity, there is another polarization essential to lovemaking. That is the heart-genital circuit.

The breasts are woman's positive pole. From them she gives the essence of her femaleness, to express the Goddess within. As the milk from her breasts provides nourishment for her infant, so the energy from those nipples nourishes her mate. Once a woman has learned to consciously pour energy out her breast, her mate, if he is sensitive, can feel the exquisite warmth of her energy as it floods him.

But man keeps his heart guarded. The heart space feels very dangerous to him. He prefers to bypass the heart and experience his sexuality only in his head and genitals. Therein lies the major issue in the battle of the sexes. Woman keeps pressing to involve man at the heart level and man avoids it with every ploy at his command.

Not until she is fully received will a woman find fulfillment. So she must be patient and slowly coax him to open his heart. She can rub circles on his chest (stimulating the heart chakra). She can stimulate his nipples, (although he may not enjoy that if his resistance is great). She can pour her love into his chest each time they embrace. Eventually she will melt his armor.

Societies in all times and places have been forgiving of men who engage in sex without love, realizing that is man's nature. But societies are universally intolerant of women who engage in sex for motives other than love. We instinctively know that woman's efforts to bring love to bear is essential to the evolution of our species. When she abandons her task, we feel a collective uneasiness. It is given to woman to teach man to love. And so it must be.

To be receptive man must surrender to his female energy, must switch his polarity and become more female. That is frightening for most men. They have been carefully trained to be manly and to hold in contempt anything "sissy." The "macho" mentality will have to give way in Tantra. Man must come to appreciate, even worship, the female principles, and be willing to experience the world in that modality.

When man finally receives in his heart, that energy goes immediately to his penis and he feels aroused. There is a direct connection between the heart chakra and the sex center. When man surrenders to the female energy for a prolonged period of time, he is transformed. His sexuality takes on a new dimension.

The penis is man's positive pole. From there he gives the energy that is the essence of his maleness. Man is very willing to give that energy, whenever and wherever possible, but once again the problem lies in the reception. Woman has been conditioned to fear pregnancy, to find this organ unappealing, to resent being used for its satisfaction. She may not realize the profound power it represents. An attitude of worship is exactly what men want and keep waiting for. Every porno movie made (calculated to satisfy men's frustrated needs) portrays a woman who adores and worships her partner's penis. How many women do that in real life?

When woman receives this energy gratefully, her heart opens even more and the energy pours from her breasts more freely. Once this circuit is flowing, two lovers can bring each other to profound satisfaction.

It is the Ultimate Destiny of woman to become the Divine Mother. From the time a girl is a tiny child, clutching a doll, she prepares to mother. The wedding ceremony in India includes a hope that the wife can become "mother" to her husband as they grow older. How many older men refer to their wives as "mother"?

It is the deepest desire of man to reenter that Cosmic Womb, the object of worship and adoration among Tantrics. The sexual act for him portrays his desire to return to the comfort of that blissful state.

For both man and woman to fulfill themselves, he must open his heart and receive nourishment from her. She must be the great Yoni that opens like a lotus to receive him.

Beginning Heart Circuit.

Since it is difficult for some men to receive through the heart, this exercise is a lovely way to ease him into receptivity.

Stimulate each other enough to allow penetration. Let woman do the moving to position herself so the solar penis shaft is rubbing on her Sacred Spot where she receives energy. He will take a nipple in his mouth and suck. This will stimulate more energy and she will feel the energy building up in her genitals as she applies the Root Lock. He can put his left hand (receiving hand) on the other nipple so nothing is wasted.

She will pull that energy up with the breath to her heart. On the exhalation she will project the energy through her nipples. If he is sensitive, he will feel a delightful rush of energy. Since the mouth is not a guarded place, and since his first instinct was to suckle for nourishment, he can receive in this way.

At some point the energy will become so intense that the woman will want to take it all the way up to the third eye several times before experiencing orgasm. This is a simple way to achieve a very long and wonderful orgasm.

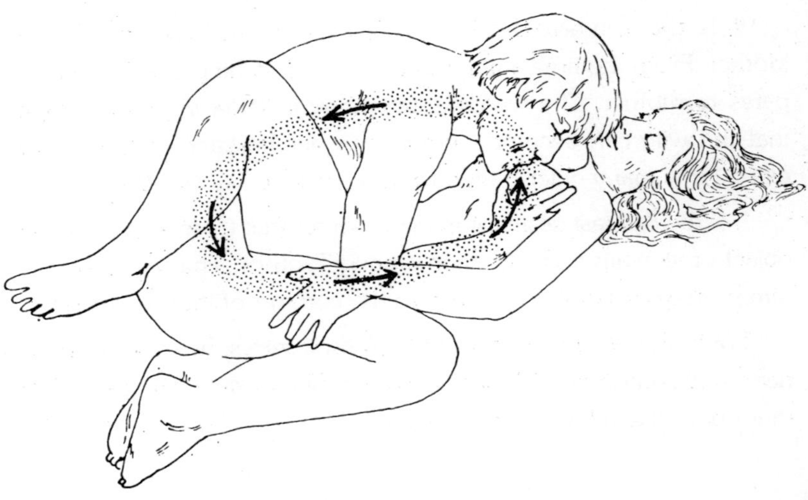

Advanced Heart Circuit.

1) Sit in Yab-Yum position, in union, with chests pressed together, arms enfolding each other.
2) Establish psychic connections first in the genitals, then in the heart, by seeing the chakras as a golden disk, then extending that light to include the partner's golden disk.
3) Establish a flow of energy. As the woman breathes out, she projects energy from her heart. Simultaneously man breathes in, receiving her energy.
4) As man breathes out he projects energy from his penis. Simultaneously the woman breathes in, receiving his energy.
5) Continue for five minutes. Let your being be filled with gratitude, knowing there is someone there to really receive what you have to give.

The feeling of gratitude is truly the key to opening the heart chakra. The word for the state of grace comes from the Latin "gratis", "thank you." The deeper your gratitude to your partner or to the Universe, the more open your heart is and the deeper your connection.

It is possible to experience orgasm at the heart chakra. The physical sensation is much like an intense full-body orgasm, but it is centered in the heart. While the emotional tone of normal orgasm is pleasure, the tone of a heart orgasm is overwhelming, uncontainable joy. There are advanced techniques to make this happen. Our experiences of it have come spontaneously.

Heart-Genital Circuit.

Prayer Mudra.

As she exhales she lowers her head to allow blood to gather in her brain. When she comes up with the Cobra Breath (or Transmutation Breath) the energy in her head floods her body. The anal contraction she performs with the inhale stimulates him and when she relaxes the contraction, the energy transfers to him.

His role is passive. He places a finger on her anus so there will be no energy loss. He does Aswini Mudra and receives the earth energy she releases to him. When that energy builds up enough pressure, he can pull it up with the Cobra Breath (or Transmutation Breath).

Laid Back.

In this position you open up the channels in both bodies. As you lay back this way, you create a very relaxed feeling. It's a low energy position and there is no thrusting movement. The man may not maintain an erection, but that doesn't matter. The energy is dispersed through the entire body/mind, not just at the genitals. This circuit is for rejuvenation.

Both are doing the anal contractions. Shiva's energy is pulled in through attraction to Shakti's magnetism. She receives his energy and lets it run through her body and back to the universe.

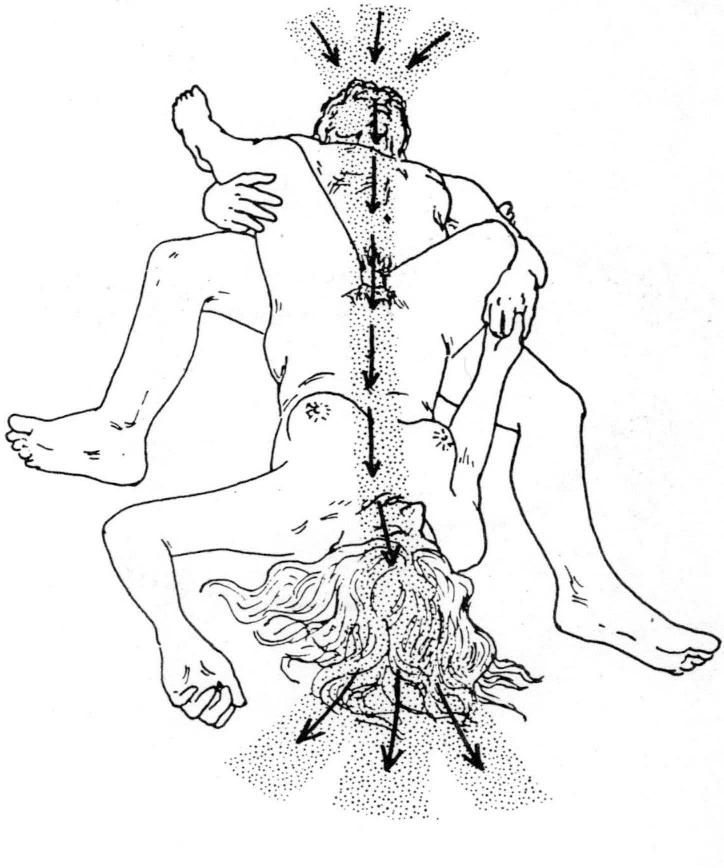

6-9 Circuit.

To be mutually engaged in oral-genital stimulation creates a circuit which stops the procreative urge. He is able to drink the dew of immortality as she manifests it. Her polarity switches in this circuit. She receives in her mouth and gives from the genitals.

In this position, or rolled onto their sides, they have full access to each other's genitals for oral and manual stimulation.

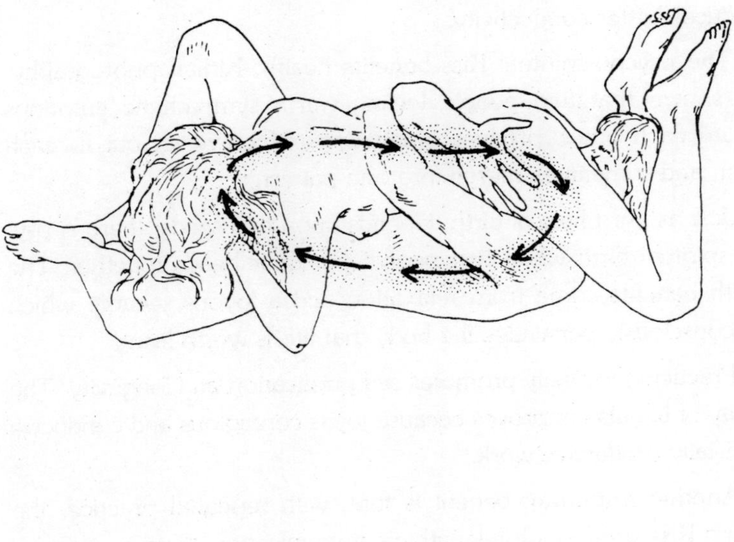

THE TANTRIC KISS

The Tantric Kiss is a Yogic greeting posture in which two people rest their foreheads together for mutual meditation. The Kiss can be done standing, reclining, or sitting in the Yab-Yum posture (limbs embracing).

Touching moistened foreheads together synchronizes brainwaves. Holding and feeling each other synchronizes heart beats. Synchronizing brain waves and heart beats has a positive correlation to ESP (extended sensory perception). Moistening the foreheads produces better conductivity.

The psycho-spiritual Kiss benefits health. Kirlian photography, has shown that two people feeling warm sympathetic emotions toward each other, produce emanations which reach out to each other, and sometimes merge into one pattern.

Just as our physical birth depends upon two seeds, there is psycho-spiritual birth when two people put their heads together. The health benefits come from relaxation and a joyous security which sub-consciously persuades the body that life is worth living.

Practicing joy daily promotes self-purification and longevity. The quality of life also improves because joy is contagious and conducive to socially productive work.

Another important benefit is that, with repeated practice, the Tantric Kiss produces a telepathic communication. Patience is necessary since it takes a while to learn each other's language.

The Tantric Kiss and Human Evolution. The psycho-sexual kiss transcends the random genetics of procreation and allows parents to design a healthy and evolved Hu-man being (Hu-man = mind of light). Repeated Tantric Kissing before conception allows the gonads to prepare harmonious seeds. After intercourse, the Tantric Kiss can psycho-kinetically fix the sperm race so that the most compatible sperm fertilizes the ovum. After conception,

Tantric Kissing promotes the best embryonic development.

By mutual concentration on desired characteristics, we can create a superior Hu-man being. Psycho-kinetic love genetics is safer and more directional than present techniques of recombinant DNA. If practiced throughout society, the Tantric Kiss would decrease the incidence of birth defects and generally lead to happier, healthier and long-lived people.

Individual Practice

1. Experiment With the Genital Circuit, visualizing energy moving back and forth in the genitals. This is, of course, far more vivid an experience with the Cobra Breath. If you haven't yet received initiation, you can practice the circuit mentally.

2. This Individual Circuit Is Really the Hong-Sau Meditation. See the correlation as you work with those two processes.

Couple Practice

Practice the Various Circuits: Heart Circuit (Beginning and Advanced), Prayer Mudra, Laid Back, 6-9 Circuits and the Tantric Kiss. Feel your minds join in directing the energy movement. Then relax and just experience it moving.

Awareness

Become Aware of Circuits That Exist between you and people in your life. Tune in to those energy exchanges clairvoyantly.

Someone who turns you on: Be aware of an energy bond at the sex chakra level.

Someone who dominates you, or you dominate them: Notice a cord joining you at the 3rd chakra.

Someone you truly love: See the energy current that flows from one heart to another.

Someone with whom you have a strong mental connection: Feel your brow centers link up when you are having a fascinating discussion.

Lesson 12

Sacred Maithuna Rite

The sacred Maithuna Rite has existed in all advanced cultures in some form, varying from culture to culture according to their traditions. This is one of the most sacred rituals that you can share with another being on this plane. If the ritual is successful it is possible to achieve enlightenment in a single practice. This is the most efficient way to the end of the path.

You have been given all the tools you need to strengthen and purify your physical and pranic bodies. If you have done your preparation and are ready, this ritual could transform your consciousness.

Many wedding ceremonies refer to becoming "one flesh." The ring finger symbolizes the lingam, the ring is the yoni. Putting the wedding ring onto the finger unites Shiva and Shakti as one. In this ritual you can begin with union of the physical bodies, then fully connect the etheric bodies, then become one mind and then no mind and then Universal Mind.

In the mystical experience we know that we are one, a single drop in the cosmic ocean. Only our "ego" keeps us feeling separate. Ego, the sense of being "I" as apart from "you" is the real barrier to fully experiencing love. The more solid the ego, the more difficult it is to unite. We're very attached to our separateness. We love to compare ourselves with other people, to judge and criticize others, to manipulate and compete with others, to blame others for our problems. All these games must be sacrificed to attain the mystical experience, for in union, no one is there. The ego must die so that you can be reborn into higher consciousness. Love only emerges out of the void where there is no "I" and no "Other."

Androgyny Is the Main Goal of Tantra. You have learned techniques to balance the male and female energies within your own body/mind. (When Ida and Pingala are in perfect balance, Kundalini rushes up Sushumna.) When you join in sexual union with your mate, you create a circuit of energy where you complement the polarities in each other's body/mind complex. Women are usually lunar, magnetic energy. They draw to them the solar, electrical impulses of men. Together they achieve a perfect balance.

When they come together consciously, as a couple making love, the polarities switch. She is no longer a typical woman and he is no longer a typical man. As he becomes more passive, she becomes more aggressive. Shiva becomes Shakti and Shakti becomes Shiva. Normally in Tantra a man has very little movement. It is the female, Shakti, that generates the energy.

After the steps of the ritual have been performed, after sexual energy has been stimulated and transmuted repeatedly, the couple lies without moving for about 30 minutes. The culmination of the ritual happens in this resolution stage. Their minds become still, their ego structures disappear, and Shiva and Shakti dissolve in mystical union with each other and with the Cosmos.

PREPARING FOR THE RITUAL

Prepare a Temple, a special space reserved only for performance of the rite. When you meditate in the same place over a period of time you produce an energy field. After a few times through the rite, just being in that setting will start the juices flowing. Always use the same incense — only sandalwood, musk or patchouli. Have a subdued light, using red, amber or violet bulbs. Provide plenty of air, a temperature that is comfortable, and two cushions. Set up an altar with two red candles, a vase of roses, pictures of the spiritual teachers you feel a connection with, or other pictures that evoke a spiritual mood. Ritual bell and dorje or a singing bowl is an elegant addition if you can manage it, and statues of various symbolic deities if that has meaning for you. Set aside at least several hours free of interruptions, all day if possible.

Prepare a Ritual Meal. On an attractive tray, place bite-sized servings of cooked meat, cooked fish and biscuit, a decanter of wine with two small wine glasses, and cardamon seeds. Leave it close to the cushions where you will be sitting.

Prepare Your Body for the rush of energy which might overtake you. We assume you have been doing your Rishi Isometrics, Nadi Kriyas Pranayama, Yantra/Mantra meditations Bandhas, Mudras, Hong Sau, and Transmutation Breath for several months. On this day do an especially deliberate sadhana with your partner.

Then take a hot bath to thoroughly clean your bodies. You can bathe together if your tub is big enough. If you have access to a hot tub near a cold pool you can produce a powerful energy charge. Soak in the hot water then go immediately into the cold. When you come close to your partner the sparks will really fly!

Take time for a leisurely full body massage. Use perfumed oils, reserving a particular scent for the Maithuna Rite which will awaken your passion in subsequent rituals. Men should wear Musk, women Patchouli, as these are the most erotic fragrances, most reminiscent of sexual secretions.

Dress in natural fibres. The synthetics disturb the flow of energy. The woman should wear a robe the color of hibiscus, the symbolic flower of Tantra.

Lovers in tantric art wear a lot of jewelry. This serves two purposes. First, dressing up in regal attire inspires an attitude of worship, sets you apart from your everyday roles. Second, the vibration of pure metals and stones can be used to amplify your energy. Solar energy comes through pure gold. Lunar energy is associated with silver. When you intermingle the two you produce a balance of energy. Copper represents the earth. The three metals together produce triangles of energy. Worn as a bracelet it helps activate the five pranic energies within the body. A ring is worn on a woman's little toe or little finger because that is connected directly to her clitoris.

The Sand Ritual is a traditional way in India to create a protective barrier around the ritual temple. Intoning the mantra OM SHIVA HUM, Shiva sprinkles a ring of sand to seal off the area, to contain the energies and ward off foreign energies. If you are more comfortable setting up a wall of white light, that will serve the same purpose. You must feel that this is a safe space, for in the Maithuna Rite you are totally open to your karma. As the circuits begin to move, both psyches will open up simultaneously. When he has finished, he sits in meditation, waiting for Shakti to enter.

PERFORMING THE RITUAL

Become Shiva and Shakti. She enters very slowly and majestically. As their eyes meet each recognizes the divinity of the other. Throughout the ritual they continue to see each other as the embodiment of Shiva and Shakti principles that reside within them. You must set aside whatever mundane conflicts are going on in the relationship. You are spending this time, not with the temporal personality of your partner, but with their divine essence. In order to recognize that essence in your partner, you must be able to recognize it in yourself.

Dance and Disrobe. Shakti moves seductively, hypnotically, allowing Shiva to enjoy the beauty of her body and her essence. She invites him into the dance, and they very slowly, provocatively, remove each other's robes. Set the erotic tone, always within the context of the spiritual awareness.

Nadabrahma

1) Burn four small candles and some musk, patchouli, or sandalwood incense. Only use these fragrances with this technique.
2) Sit facing each other, nude, with your hands crossed, holding your partner's hands.

3) Cover yourselves completely with a bed sheet.
4) Close your eyes and begin humming together for ten minutes. After a minute or two, your breathing and humming will unify.
5) As you hum you will feel your energies merge.

Ritual Meal. Each item in this sacrament has symbolic meaning. All together they represent the Universe. This ritual served as shock therapy for the Indian people because they were required to participate in five forbidden practices: eating meat, fish, aphrodisiac grains, wine, and sexual union. Meat represents the animal world from which we came. First he gives her a morsel of meat, placing it in her mouth as he intones the mantra "Pat." That is a technique to infuse his energy into the morsel, and into her body. She places a morsel in his mouth, with the same mantra. Then they sip just a taste of wine - symbolic of the blood of life. By participating in this "blood" ritual you are uniting your two nervous systems. Taken in moderation the wine loosens inhibition and elevates consciousness.

Fish is symbolic of the sexual energy within our bodies, the water element. They offer each other a morsel with the mantra, and again share a sip of wine. Each step is followed by a meditation. You must be conscious of what you are doing. As you ingest each substance, fill your consciousness with the taste of it so each morsel tastes divine to you. Tantra works through the five senses. Each sense produces an explicit high if used consciously.

The grain symbolizes the earth. They eat and sip and meditate. Then they open a cardamon seed. Its two halves symbolize the male and female halves of a total being. It also sweetens the breath and gives you a natural high.

Tantric Energy Transference

Shiva projects his energy into Shakti and then she projects her energy into him to achieve balance. They use the words of power to invoke Shiva consciousness and make it manifest.

1) Sit in an easy pose, nude, knees touching.
2) Visualize a golden circle of light the size of thumb and forefinger joined. Place inside a glowing red dot (Bindu).

In the following steps, to help concentration, anoint each body part with a drop of oil as you chant the mantra. Shiva (man) should anoint first, then Shakti (woman).

3) Touch the Third Eye and project the image of the circle to your partner as you mentally chant OM—SHIVA—HUM.
4) Touch the left ear lobe. Chant OM—SHIVA—HUM (to activate Ida).
5) Touch the right ear lobe. Chant OM—SHIVA—HUM (to activate Pingala).
6) Touch the left nipple. Chant OM—SHIVA—HUM.
7) Touch the right nipple. Chant OM—SHIVA—HUM.
8) Touch the navel. Chant OM—SHIVA—HUM.
9) Touch the clitoris (or penis). Chant OM—SHIVA—HUM. Honor the Divine Yoni or Shiva Lingam.

When you finish, lie down together (Shakti on top) and feel the energy connecting you to each other.

Foreplay

Now lose your self in foreplay, in erotic massage, touching, kissing, sucking, stimulating in whatever way you enjoy. Let this go on for half an hour or until both are aroused. Don't allow yourself to climax. Just let the energy build up and then transmute it throughout the body.

The Holy Kiss

When you are ready to come into union, honor the sacredness of each other's sexuality. Shiva bows before Shakti and kisses her feet and then her vulva, portal to the Cosmic Yoni. Shakti bows before Shiva and kisses the Shivalingam until it is fully erect.

As you come into the classical Yab-Yum position, he gently slides his Lingam deep within her, and her Yoni throbs in welcome. Create a very slow thrusting rhythm.

Continue until you are very close to a climax then perform the Tantric Kiss to synchronize both brain hemispheres so you become in essence one.

The Tantric Kiss

1) Sitting in Yab-Yum, in union, do Khechari Mudra, inhaling deeply through the mouth.
2) Do a chin lock, just gently to lock in the energy, and touch foreheads. Focus your attention on the Third Eye.
3) Contract the anus three times.
4) Sit back, take a sniff of air that goes into the Ajna.
5) Exhale, chanting EE - AH - OH as the energy moves down.

The Tantric Kiss produces a psychic experience, a blue or white light. When you exhale you feel a surge of energy moving down the spine. This will balance the solar and lunar energies, neutralizing the polarities, to allow a melting into Ultimate Universal Unity.

Tantra Maithuna

Tuning to each other at ever more subtle levels, our Holy Couple is now ready to begin the final process.

Shakti lies on her back and Shiva lies next to her on his left side.

She puts her left leg between his legs and her right leg over his hip in a comfortable scissors position.

He inserts his Lingam into her Yoni.

There is no more physical movement, only meditation.

Their breath comes into its own rhythm.

Each visualizes a disc of light encompassing both genitals.

With their two minds working as one they begin the Cobra Breath.

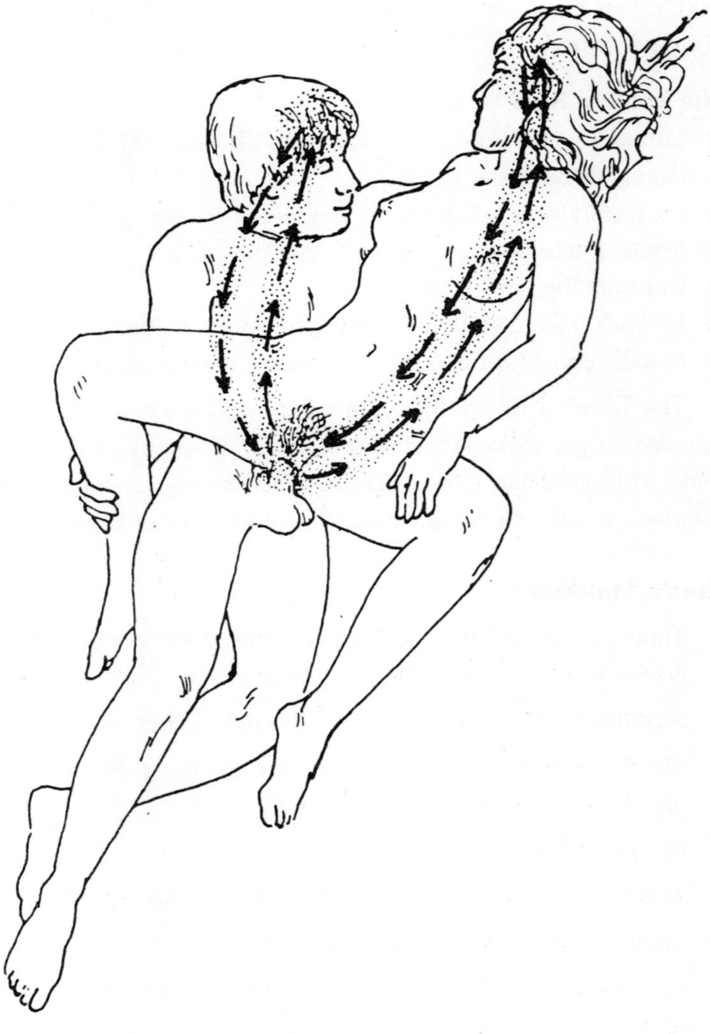

As Shiva exhales deeply, he imagines he is pushing the light energy from his sex center through Shakti's body to the crown of her head.

At the same time Shakti inhales deeply, imagining she is pulling the energy up from her sex center to her crown chakra.

Shiva inhales, pulling the energy back from his partner's crown through her sex center to his sex center and all the way up to his crown.

Shakti exhales and pictures the energy flowing from the crown of her head through both sex centers and up to the crown of his head.

One is inhaling and the other is exhaling as the energy flows back and forth between them for several minutes.

Now they both relax the imagery and tune in to the feeling in their bodies. If the energy is flowing freely, waves of orgasmic pleasure course through their bodies.

They enter a meditative state and continue for 30-35 minutes.

At that time, a transformation occurs in their nervous systems.

There is a blinding flash of awareness as Shakti's energy infuses Shiva's consciousness.

They become one in a moment beyond time,

in the eternal now, beyond the senses and the mind,

absorbed in the infinite Truth that passeth all understanding,

where there are no longer lovers, there is only love.

CONCLUSION

In this course you have learned some of the basic "secrets" of Tantric Kriya Yoga, about the energy centers in our bodies, and the energies that exist within and outside of us that are available for our use. You now have enough knowledge about this system to use it in your daily lives.

Through the use of Tantric Kriya Yoga techniques you too can develop healing powers, psychic abilities and other phenomena which the Yogis have been credited with possessing. The only limitation is your commitment to practice.

In the Saraswati Order we honor Saraswati, the goddess of learning, arts, music, and prosperity. We teach techniques that will bring forth creativity you had never thought possible. Transmuting sexual energy with the Cobra Breath stimulates the frontal lobes of the brain where creativity begins. Our students suddenly find themselves writing music and poetry, eager to paint and to undertake new ventures.

The ultimate gain to be had from these techniques is the ability to flow with the universal stream of life, to relax to adversity so that you may handle challenges smoothly and calmly, and to receive an inner understanding of the laws of existence. Then you may not only tune into the mysteries of life, but plug into them and become a functioning part of the whole in a conscious manner, instead of feeling like you are being tossed about by the fateful throes of life.

You can be your own fortune teller, your own healer, your own psychological advisor. Where you may have found only heartache or disappointment in your relationships, you can truly develop the ability to "live and let live," to understand where others fit into the scheme of things, to allow things to be the way they are.

When you are able to flow with life, life will also flow with you. Successes will come more easily; failures will no longer be as devastating as they once were. And failure comes much less frequently because you will have the tools that will allow you to see more clearly where the pitfalls are in this life—and where the rainbows will appear.

GLOSSARY

Sanskrit Pronunciation: a = ah, e = eh, i = ee, o= oh, u = oo.

AGNI: the fire God of the Hindu pantheon.

AJNA: the sixth chakra known as the third eye. This center represents objectivity.

ANAHATA: the fourth chakra, located at the heart, center of devotion.

APANA: the excretory aspect of the five pranas.

ASANA: in Hatha Yoga, a physical posture.

ATMAN: the esssence of perfection hidden within all creatures.

BANDHA: a muscular lock.

BIJI: seed or root sounds.

BINDU: a state of balanced awareness; the moon chakra; the point on the crown of the head where the soul enters and leaves the body; the center of the Yantra card; a drop of semen.

CHAKRA: literally "wheel." These are astral, not physical, vital centers in the body located in positions corresponding to the endrocrine glands of the body and along the spine.

GURU: dispeller of ignorance. A teacher.

GYANA MUDRA: symbol of wisdom. Position of hand with tips of index fingers touching base (or tip) of thumb.

HAMSA: the swan, a symbol of spiritual liberation.

HONG-SAU: "I am he."

HATHA: the sanskrit stems "ha," meaning sun, and "tha," meaning moon, joined. Symbolic of the soul and body of the human being.

IDA: the left hand or negative pole of the three principal nadis, running parallel along the side of Sushumna, within the spinal column and opposed to Pingala.

JALANDHARA BANDHA: the chin lock.

KHECHARI MUDRA: posture in which the tongue is curled back into the throat in order to block the openings of the nasal passage, pharynx, and trachea.

KRIYA: internal cleansing process; action.

KUNDALINI: Cosmic energy that activates the consciousness.

LINGAM: the male sex organ.

MAHA: great.

MAITHUNA: sexual union.

MANIPURA: the third chakra located at the solar plexus. This center represents power.

MANTRA: a word used for its vibratory effect on the human being.

MAYA: illusion.

MEDULLA OBLONGATA: the area in the body at the upper neck where the spinal column and brain meet.

MUDRA: position taken by fingers or limbs used to activate or connect electrical currents in the body.

MULADHARA: the first chakra located at the base of the spine. This center represents the urge for survival.

NADIS: astral channels which correspond to nerves of the body.

NIRVANA: extinction of self will.

PINGALA: the right hand or positive pole of the three principal nadis.

PRANA: vital energy of the universe absorbed by the body from the air and natural foods. The life force of the human being.

PRANAYAMA: yogic energy control exercise.

SAHASRARA: the seventh chakra located at the top of the head. This is the thousand petaled lotus which represents cosmic consciousness.

SAMADHI: the deep state of meditation.

SAMARASA: superconscious state. Also called Cosmic Consciousness

SAMSKARA: a deep mental impression produced by past experiences.

SHAKTI: the feminine aspect of kundalini, kinetic energy.

SHIVA: the masculine aspect of kundalini, static energy.

SIDDHI: a para-normal power.

SUSHUMNA: central pole of the main nadis; the pole of enlightenment. It corresponds to the spinal cord within the vertebral column.

SUTRA: a book composed of short sentenced thoughts.

SVADHISTHANA: the second chakra located at the genital area. This is the center which represents sexual arousal and sexual energy.

UDDIYANA BANDHA: abdominal lock.

VASANA: habits, desires and tendencies.

VISUDDHI: the fifth chakra located at the throat. This center represents creativity and communication.

YANTRA: a visual representation of vibrational frequencies.

YOGA: to yoke into union.

YONI: the female sex organ.

YUGA: age or epoch. This is the Kali Yuga.

TANTRIC PRACTICES

Lesson 1. Enlightenment Through Tantric Kriya Yoga

Lesson 2. The Breath and Pranic Energy

Lesson 3. Asanas: Charging the Body With Pranic Energy

Lesson 4. Cosmic Unity of Opposites

Lesson 11. Positions and Circuit

Lesson 12. Sacred Maithuna Ritual

Index of Techniques

BOOKS OF RELATED INTEREST

BEATING TANTRA AT ITS OWN GAME: Spiritual Sexuality — *Arthur Lytle*

Tantra introduces a middle path, extending the delights of male-female coupling into rarely attained Bliss. Through integrating all levels of human consciousness, the usual short period of arousal, climax, and afterglow is extended for hours at a time without debilitation. This text lucidly discusses the 'What', the 'How', and the 'Why' of exercises capable of transforming sensuality and sexuality into Spirituality.

81-7822-148-9

A METHOD FOR TANTRIC BLISS: The Ipsalu Formula — *Bodhi Avinasha*

A Method for Tantric Bliss, presents a practical approach to spiritual awakening, leading to a joyful experience of who you really are, and your oneness with all things, your bliss.

Created on a solid foundation of ancient principles and practices with deep psychological insights, The Ipsalu Formula works for everyone who practices it.

81-7822-189-6

TANTRA WITHOUT TEARS — *Christopher S. Hyatt & S. Jason Black*

This book gives you the understanding and ability to use certain symbols, sounds and images that you will find in more conventional and classical texts. In other words, as well as an instructional text, it is also a jumping off point for those who wish to pursue the original Eastern material.

This book tells one how to achieve and utilize power to meet one's own needs and suit one's own ends.

81-7822-027-x

TANTRIC SEX: A Unique Guide to Love and Sexual Fulfilment — *Diana Richardson*

How did we lose the art of keeping love fresh and new long after the honeymoon is over? Diana Richardson found that the ancient practice of Tantra, with its unique, intelligent approach to sex, had the effect of enhancing intimacy and deepening love. Here she has adapted Tantra for modern lovers in a practical sympathetic way. *Tantric Sex* can transform your experience into a more sensual, loving and fulfilling one.

The material appears in three sections which look at the divine potential of sex and love; practical body-oriented suggestions, and crucial aspects of sex and sexuality.

81-7822-188-8

EROS, CONSCIOUSNESS AND KUNDALINI: Deepening Sensuality Through Tantric Celibacy and Spiritual Intimacy — *Stuart Sovatsky*

Tantric celibacy is based upon a profoundly spiritual understanding of bodily maturation and Eros that includes definitive stages of psychophysical development beyond genital puberty.

As a spiritual phenomenon, kundalini helps our basic sense of identity mature from one connected to limited egos to one that is based in our eternal souls. The goal of tantric celibacy is not merely to live a contented celibate life and gain enhanced health and intimacy, but also reach a gradual awakening of the supremely creative force.

81-7822-179-9

TAOIST BEDROOM SECRETS: Tao Chi Kung: Sexual-Therapeutic Exercises for Enjoyment, Health, and Rejuvenation — *Master Chian Zettnersan*

The book teaches to learn more about the deep sexual wisdom of Love. According to the traditional teaching, the Taoist bedroom secrets are the root of human happiness. They are based on the foundation of the ancient Chinese procedures of diagnosis, therapy, and treatment. This fascinating work focuses on the *"jade stem"* and the *"jade gate,"* which symbolize the exchange of masculine and feminine energy.

81-7822-133-0

MOTHER OF THE UNIVERSE: Visions of the Goddess and Tantric Hymns of Enlightenment — *Lex Hixon*

The Great Mother is humanity's most primordial, pervasive, and fruitful image of reality. Either secretly or openly, she appears with extra-ordinary power, wisdom, and tenderness at the core of every noble culture. She illuminates the entire universe because she is not some local or limited goddess but our Universal Mother. She expresses herself fluently through and within every sacred tradition, without needing to call attention to her feminine nature.

81-7822-190-x

FENG SHUI FOR THE BODY: Balancing Body and Mind for a Healthier Life — *Daniel Santos*

This breakthrough book applies the principles of Feng Shui, the ancient Chinese art of energy flow, to the most intimate house we inhabit—the human body. Daniel Santos shows us how to use the Four Motions—body movement, breath, eye movement, and sound—to maximize the flow of healthful life energy. Postures, simple exercises, and innovative meditations, as well as a fascinating story of personal discovery, offer fresh insights into body-mind healing.

81-7822-012-1

FENG SHUI FOR RELATIONSHIP: The Yin & Yang of Love — *Shan-Tang Tsu*

Love is a process of dynamic balance of Yin and Yang energies. Love is the force that shapes the entire universe. The interaction of Yin and Yang is not an abstraction; it is the experience of love in all its forms.

This book is a fresh look at love and what *we can do to attract love.* Author Shan-Tung Hsu combines his knowledge of traditional Feng Shui and Taoist philosophy in this simple, direct guide to healthy and harmonious relationships.

This book goes beyond the basics, showing you how to use Taoist and Feng Shui principles in all areas of your life to attract lasting love and happiness.

81-7822-197-7